NAKED

PICTURES

OF

FAMOUS

PEOPLE

NAKED PICTURES

OF FAMOUS PEOPLE

JON STEWART

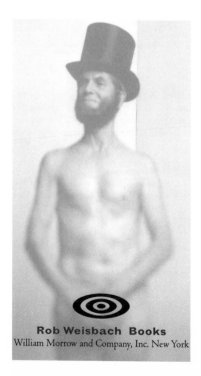

Rob Weisbach Books
William Morrow and Company, Inc. New York

Published by Rob Weisbach Books
An Imprint of William Morrow and Company, Inc.
1350 Avenue of the Americas, New York, N.Y. 10019

ISBN 0-688-15530-8

Library of Congress Cataloging-in-Publication Data has been applied for.

Printed in the United States of America

First Edition

1 2 3 4 5 6 7 8 9 10

BOOK DESIGN BY LEAH S. CARLSON

For my loves—Tracey, Stan, and Shamsky.
No offense, Sportscenter.

ACKNOWLEDGMENTS

The following people contributed love, inspiration, support, advice, therapy, friendship, research, money, criticism, pressure, name-calling, threats of physical violence or genetic material. The book could not have been completed without them, and yet, even with them, I still missed deadlines.

Marian Leibowitz, Donald Leibowitz, Larry, Shelly, Benjamin and Abbey Leibowitz, Nathan Laskin, Bob and Mary Spiegel, James Dixon, Jimmy Miller, Lee Stollman, Jeff Garlin, Matt Labov, Peter Huyck, Alex Gregory, Adam Resnick, Michael Shore, Kyle Heller, Paul Nelson, Bobby Cohen, Michael Klein, Denis Leary, Diane Dwyer, Chris McShane, Jill Liederman and Dan Strone.

Special mention of thanks to my editor, Rob Weisbach. Without his skilled and persistent knowledge I never would have developed gastrointestinal problems.

Tracey, I cannot express how much your love and support have meant. All I can do is promise not to wake you at three in the morning to try.

CONTENTS

BREAKFAST AT KENNEDY'S

DURING THE SPRING of 1935 I had the good fortune of making as my close acquaintance none other than John F. (Jack) Kennedy. Jack and his roommate Lemoyne Billings (LeMoan, Jack would say with an impish grin) were sixth-formers at the prestigious boarding school Choate, where I was a struggling fourth-former. Jack was top dog at the school, much beloved for his lightning wit and easy way with the ladies, but one sensed a sadness about him. A sadness that came from being an outcast, the only Catholic at an all-Protestant boarding school. That's where Jack and I bonded. I was the only Jew. My father ran the commissary so I was allowed to attend school there. My room, or the Yeshiva, as Jack called it (he really wasn't prejudiced and would often defend me to the others as a "terrific yid"), was a meeting place and a hotbed for hatching great pranks ... I'm sure the ample supply of brisket and white-fish from Dad helped. Whatever it was, Jack and I bonded and that spring break he invited Lem and me to visit with his family in Hyannis. Lem, because he was Jack's best friend. "Big, ugly, retarded, chickenshit Lem," Jack would winningly prod. And me—I guess because of our outcast bond ... and our similar views on family and politics ... and I had a car.

I'm glad I kept this journal. I hope it gives the reader some sense of ... not President Kennedy, not Camelot, but the happy-go-lucky boy we knew—Jack.

APRIL 9, 1935

Trip gets off to a rocky start. I argued terribly with Father over the use of the family's Hudson. It's our only car and my father felt he might need it to rush my younger brother to the doctor. He recently contracted a form of typhus and the hospital is a good ten miles from campus. The argument was quite heated. A "kikefight," Jack would expertly chide. Although my father forbade me to take the car, Jack showed me how to start it without the keys and off we went. Any ambivalent feelings I had were assuaged when Jack put his arm around me and said he admired my pluck. "The Zippy Zionist," he would say, smartly using alliteration.

Hyannis is worth the trouble, though. I can't believe only one family lives here, but, oh, what a family. There must be hundreds of them. It's like a Catholic Oz. Mr.

and Mrs. K weren't there to greet us, but I could've sworn I saw Ava Gardner in the back kitchen cleaning fish.

I also experienced my first Kennedy family tradition!!! They tell me it's a welcoming ritual given to all first timers called a "clogging." Jack initiates the festivity with a high-pitched Gaelic cry and then the brood is on you. It's great fun, and although it appears young Bobby broke my nose with his knee and there are some bite marks on my kidneys from the girls, Dr. Salk said there is no internal bleeding. I hope not. Jack says there's a sailing race scheduled in the morning and I don't want to miss it.

P.S. The place is so big I've been given virtually an entire wing of the house. Jack spontaneously dubbed it Dachau, and the whole gang joined in the fun, saying if I so much as wandered into their end of the compound I would be castrated.

APRIL 10

Whatta day!! Where to start?! Woken up at 6:30 A.M. by the maid, a beautiful woman who I swear looks just like Fay Wray but insisted I refer to her as "Number 3." Thought I was the first one up but it turns out I'd already missed the boat race as well as a bakeoff, boxing match and aeronautics seminar given by none other than Lindy himself. This crowd gets things done. Jack took one glance at my late arrival and keenly dubbed me "one lazy cock-sucker." Hearing the rib, Mr. K parried that he "could make a million dollars in the time it took me to take a shit!!" Algonquin, table for two, please!!

One fly in today's whirlwind ointment: Apparently two Kennedy boys drowned during the sailing race: Phil, twelve, and Boris, eight. But Mrs. K gave birth while attending morning church services so everyone's considering the day a wash. (She went into labor during the sermon and had the baby in time for its first communion.) Jack says that's no great shakes. One time Mrs. K took a flight from New York to Miami, got pregnant during beverage service and had the baby before the dinner had been cleared. She's hearty!! The baby's name is Sean and Mr. K gave him to Lindy in appreciation for the exciting flights around Nantucket Bay. Smarts *and* generosity!!!

Feel bad for three-year-old Teddy. Not only did he lose the boxing match and was forced to sit naked on a block of ice, but it appears his adultlike head is too large for his preschool body. As he walks, he takes to dragging his head on the ground behind him, like an exhausted Santa Claus with the last of his toys. Mr. K had a training wheel apparatus constructed to keep Teddy's head aloft while he walks, but it appears to cause him some discomfort.

I'm looking forward to tonight. Kitty Brookstone, Muffy Aldridge and Vagina Johnson are in town (one for each of us!) and Jack's throwing a costume ball. The theme is the Marx Brothers' *A Night at the Opera* and I'm going as a guy who goes to the opera. My costume's perfect, right down to the shoes!! Even little Teddy's got a date. He's got a thing going with an older woman (a six-year-old, har-

har). He looked so cute as he went to pick her up on his chauffeured tricycle. Mothers, lock up your daughters!!!!

Well, I better get crackin'. They say it's my turn to help put in the irrigation system for the south fields of the Hyannis compound. *"Arbeiten sind Freiheit,"* says Mr. K. I want to be sure I have time to be done and cleaned up before dinner. Mrs. K is a stickler for tidiness and, although she doesn't eat or speak with the family, I'm told it's unwise to cross her rules.

APRIL 11

Oh well, you know what Steinbeck says about the best laid plans . . . Apparently I missed quite an evening last night. Word is the costume party was a grand success and the ladies were every bit the temptresses. Of course positioning for their affections would have been useless, as they all fell quite hard for our boy Jack—who went as Harpo no less!!!! He bagged three luscious coeds without uttering a word. When I complimented him on the feat he retorted enchantingly, "What choice did they have? This grotesque, Neanderthal, shit stain, open sore of a man"—pointing to Lem—"or moi?" Lem and I laughed so hard we nearly choked.

I hadn't been able to attend the party, after badly miscalculating the time needed for an irrigation project of that scope, as well as the temperament of my fellow workers. (Note: The Chinese are well mannered but don't care if in fact you *do* know the price of tea in their country or that Jewish families traditionally eat their foods every Christmas Eve.) I passed out before they could remove the pickax from beneath my shoulder blades, but I'm told very little structural damage was done. Although I did overhear some amazement at how so little a man could contain so much blood. Jack was kind enough to wander over to the infirmary to check on my condition. He kept the nursing staff in stitches by reaching into the wound and pretending to feel around for a watch he lost. It was a real picker upper!!

Jack and Lem are just now leaving to get ready for tonight's Hyannis event, a costume ball with a New Deal theme. Lem's going as the Tennessee Valley Authority and Jack as a wheelchair. Mr. K is fixing all the boys Penicillin Martinis in expectation. Optimists all. All except young Bobby, who has been holding his hand over an open flame since Wednesday night as penance for incorrectly answering his father's query "Who is the finance minister of Japan?" Bobby thought Keisuko Okada when it is apparently Korekiyo Takahashi (Okada being prime minister). An innocent schoolboy mistake, but Bobby's quite hard on himself.

One down note. The girl Teddy took out last night is missing and Teddy himself showed up only this morning, covered in seaweed and looking quite bedraggled. Teddy remembers drinking some fermented lemonade the night before and little else; meanwhile they continue to drag the bay looking for his tricycle (an antique from Florence, Italy!!).

All is forgiven. Although Teddy was punished for missing the morning's whittling contest by having his head glued to a tugboat's hull as it made its morning rounds. P.S. Joe Jr. won the contest by whittling a life-size replica of Bruno Hauptmann in the electric chair... out of soap... AND IT WORKED!!! Rupert Kennedy, fourteen, was killed during the demonstration but Mrs. K gave birth to triplets at her afternoon canasta game. One of the triplets had webbed feet and was whisked away. I guess for some physical therapy. Mr. K joked that he wouldn't tolerate imperfection and put an exclamation point on the gag by punching Lem in the face.

Oh well, that's all for now as my arm and back are throbbing a bit and I see my sponge bath has arrived. My nurse is a large man with sad eyes who bears an uncanny resemblance to Herbert Hoover but insists I call him "Pete." If I permit myself one complaint in an otherwise glorious stay... I've been here almost three days and have yet to have something to eat. . . .

APRIL 12

(*Editor's note: This entry is scrawled on a piece of dilapidated cardboard in what appears to be blood.*)

It is near midnight and I fear this may be my last entry— ever. I have committed a terrible transgression and if I am to die because of it, perhaps it is justified. If only I weren't so damned selfish. My injuries had left me in a somewhat weakened state and rather than tough it out, which is unfortunately not my nature (as Jack once aptly quipped at me while delivering a winning address in front of the student body, "Shut up, you big pussy!"), I went in search of food. Unwilling to abandon a search that had given no yield, I entered an area of the house which was obviously not meant for guests. It was a darkened bunker beneath the stairs leading up to the servants' quarters. Having lifted the heavy metal lever locking the doors and setting in motion the large mechanical winch which keeps them closed (no easy task with only one good arm), I ventured in, doors creaking closed behind me. What I see now is a nightmare appealing only to the most hardened Coney Island carny. A huddled mass of moaning and dilapidated "humanity." To my left vicious Siamese twins nip at my clothes; an elephant man with a demonic Irish twinkle in his eye bellows in my face; and on my right a corpulent mass with what appears to be an ass for a face threatens to drown me in its secretions. Incredibly, these ghouls all angrily claim to be full-blooded members of the family living upon these luxurious grounds, the Kennedys. They don't recognize the dementia of this statement or Mr. K's charity in assuming their custody. Although there are a few lost souls here whose only deformity appears to be a receding hairline, lazy eye or perhaps a weak chin, I think it best not to challenge their assertion as it appears to antagonize them. I must go. I'll need my good arm to deflect the attention of three approaching dwarflike lobster people who, with agitated movement of their fins, have taken a sudden interest in my activities . . . Please tell my fami—

APRIL 18

HALLELUJAH!!! Salvation is mine. This morning the doors creaked open and a bald German man who claimed to be the director Erich von Stroheim, but is obviously just a man Friday for the Kennedys, came to caretake the ward. I was able to sneak past him, as the powerful fire-hose he was wielding proved a convenient distraction. Further good news. One of the servants had mistakenly placed the unfortunate webbed triplet in with the bunker miscreants. In the confusion of my escape I was able to wrest her from the smothering attention of an eight-breasted wolf woman.

Blessings to Mr. K. He is willing to not involve the authorities in my careless trespassing in exchange for my father's company. He even gave me the little pixie I pulled from the hellish pit that almost claimed my life. I am hoping the introduction of this little cherub will ease the blow of my younger brother's passing. He died on mile seven of the ten-mile walk to the hospital.

Back at school now, where Lem and Jack made quite a fuss over my return. Understandably fearing the worst, Jack had sold my possessions and bought shoes with the proceeds. He had planned on including them in a time capsule to memorialize me. My eyes fill just thinking about it.

I'm still a bit tired and there has been a bit of damage done to my appendages (the incessant gnawing of my recent company) but doctors say it's nothing sulfur treatments and some long-sleeved shirts and knickers won't hide. Jack caught sight of the damage and bewitchingly dubbed me "the kosher hors d'oeuvre." It's been a helluva vacation. Here's to Palm Beach in winter!!! I can't wait!!!

A VERY HANSON CHRISTMAS, 1996–1999

December 15, 1996

HEY Y'ALL!

Greetings and happy tidings to all, in this the beautiful season to celebrate the Savior's birth. The tree is up and the Christmas Ham is awaiting my apricot glaze, so once again it's time to check in for our yearly Hanson Family update. A promise from the heart to keep this year's newsletter as brief as possible (I hear you sighing, Uncle Jack! Just kidding, I can't hear you!). It's hard to believe that a year has passed since my last correspondence. Time sure flies when Jesus is flying the plane! It's a crisp afternoon here in Sooner Country. Gary and the boys are off hunting snow rabbits so the girls and I broke out the old Smith-Corona to fill everyone in. Don't worry, Peg, there's a

Pumpkin Pie waiting for my men when they return—hopefully with a fresh kill.

We're awaiting a wonderful Christmas. As is our family tradition, no gifts are exchanged but all the children will prepare a drawing, poem or play. This year's theme is Genesis. The girls are painting a beautiful mural of God's creation of man, using only the juices of fruit they grew themselves. Isaac and Taylor are preparing a heartwarming skit on the Garden of Eden (Taylor makes a beautifully innocent Eve) and little Zach, well, let's just say shouting "Let there be light" and Clapping the Clapper on and off doesn't show great inspiration. It doesn't matter. We love all our children equally, and still believe greatly in last year's Christmas theme, "Abortion Is Murder."

Some Hanson Highlights: Gary's working on a book about our methods of teaching the children called *All I Needed to Know I Learned in Kindergarten, at Home with My Parents, Who Taught Me Better Than Any Government-Run Public School That Denies Prayer Could*. The girls once again won the yearly Hanson Home School Science Fair. They devised a method for testing the bacterial content of foods using only Litmus Paper, Paper Clips and a homemade Centrifuge. These girls are going places! The boys did well too. They built a mobile depicting the fallacy of evolution. As for Zach, well, let's just say sneaking something into our dinner and waiting to see if anyone would eat it and become ill didn't impress these judges. But we love all our children equally and hope one day Zach will tell us what it was, and why I can no longer hold down solid foods.

In Hanson Sports News, it was a very good year. The Hansons played a very strong schedule, going head to head with the only other Home School Team in the area, the Jurgensons. It was great fun.

Oh, before I forget, the boys continue with their little music project. They recently played the Devlin County Pan-Asian Wet and Wild Jamboree for Vietnamese Exiles. I don't want to go into too much detail, in this, the season of good tidings, but the crafty little Asian gentleman who organized the fair tried to cheat the boys out of their $50 performance fee. We nearly came to blows over the matter, but eased off when both parties quoted the same piece of foreboding scripture at the same time. I can't say I condone the boys' interest in this pursuit of popular music, but as I always say, "Encouragement is next to Charity, which is next to Faith, which is next to Cleanliness . . . and we all know what that's next to."

Jesus loves you,
Eileen and Gary Hanson and the Hanson Family

P.S. Any donations to the charity to help that poor boy in our neighborhood with the cleft lip would be greatly appreciated. We've raised some money, but he still looks odd when he eats in public, which is often. Remember, Charity begins at home, which, as you know, is where we have our school.

December 25, 1997

Dear ~~Hanson Super Fan~~ Friends and Family,

Hey everybody! It's that time of year again! And what an amazing year it's been. I apologize for the Fan Club stationery, but it's all I could find. Normally I would just ask Carmen where she put the newsletter paper, but I gave her the day off. Most of her family is somewhere in South America, but bless her heart, she still seemed set on not working the holiday. Although I'm sure you could make a case that that's when I would need her most.

I feel bad about the stationery even though I'll bet none of you care. I'll bet you're just impressed that with all the amazing things happening to our family I still make a point of personally sending out the yearly holiday update. I agree! That is exactly what I told Gary, who was of the mind that if you all really need information, you can visit our official Web site like everybody else. But that's crazy. Being stars doesn't mean we can't take the time to stay in touch with our friends and family. By the way, the unofficial sites are *not* sanctioned and contain a great deal of fabricated information. I can't stress that enough. Our official site has received over two million hits to date!!

You're probably saying to yourself, "Wow, that must be making them a fortune!" You would think!! Although perhaps you are not taking into consideration a poorly negotiated contract that paid a one-time up-front fee and neglected any back end or merchandising considerations.

But you know our Gary. I think when the Lord was passing out business acumen, Gary was downstairs getting good hair. Of course you can't tell that to Gary. I guess he figures his year and a half of technical school and previous work experience selling homemade knickknacks at mall art fairs qualifies him to manage a world-famous band.

A big "I'm sorry" on behalf of Gary, the boys and myself for not being at Ned and Irene's annual family re-union picnic. The girls told Carmen it was a hoot. Unfortunately that was the weekend before the Grammys and as you might imagine we were swamped. While the boys were sad to miss Irene's annual mock apple pie, their dinner with Fiona Apple softened the blow. I had heard through the grapevine that Irene was a little bent out of shape. I'm sure that's not true because Irene and Ned are God-fearing people and very aware that envy is a sin.

Ooops! Please excuse the sloppy penmanship. I'm jotting this update from the back of a Limousine the boys bought me for Christmas, and the slick leather interior doesn't offer great stability. Lincoln, my driver, and I have developed a very funny joke where he calls me Miss Daisy and I pretend that's my real name.

Well, enough chatter, I better have Lincoln take me home. The boys and Gary are in Düsseldorf, but Zach still likes me to spend at least six hours a day in his room, cleaning the shag carpet, strand by strand, with my teeth. Anything for my little angel, because, as I always say, I love all my three boys equally.

It's been a wild year. The Lord sure works in myste-rious ways, or as I like to say, "What a long strange trip it's been!"

Jesus loves us,
Eileen, Gary, Zach, Taylor and Isaac
(collectively known as Hanson)

P.S. You can stop sending money for the ~~gimp~~ boy with the Cleft Lip. It turns out we had enough money left over from just one mall show to ~~ship~~ help him and his entire family off to Nebraska.

December 28, 1999

To Whom It May Concern,

HO, HO, HO! Zach has Herpes. There. Are you Happy now? You try controlling an eleven-year-old multi-millionaire with a hard-on for strippers. For those of you wondering about last year's newsletter, there wasn't one. If you must know, I was at a retreat in Hazelden, Minnesota, and they didn't allow pens, pencils or any other sharp im-plements for that matter. It's been quite a ride ... quite a ... I sit here, alone in my Hotel suite. Pen in one hand, bottle of Glenlivet in the other. A gun at my feet. Darkness all around me ...

First of all, to all you Nosy Parkers in the crowd. I did not embezzle money from my family, I don't give a rat's ass what that judge says. I am their manager ... co-manager ...

was their co-manager. I had every right to that money. I gave birth to those boys. What did Gary do? His three minutes of dirty business? Foreplay?! Please. Whispering "The Bible says be Fruitful and Multiply" before ejaculating and passing out isn't foreplay. Seven times I allowed that man to sully me ... seven times.

I'm tired ... so very tired. Someone had to have some fiscal responsibility. Christ! Do you know what Taylor and Isaac did on their big "Africa Tour"? Sat in a hotel restaurant ordering Lasagna made from 1,000-dollar bills and White Tiger's Blood. Not all the time, of course. No, sometimes they would lock themselves in their hotel rooms doing what looked and tasted like high-grade Brazilian Heroin. Where was their father, you might ask? Oh I don't know, maybe shacked up in some Backwater Indonesian Fuckee Suckee bar. Maybe it's just me, but I still believe in a thing called Statutory Rape Laws.

You think I'm bitter? You think I'm beaten? You think I might take the pills I have in my hand, wash them down with Scotch and glide off into a world of euphoria where all my pain will cease? HA! No, this old girl has some fight in her yet. Believe it!! I know things. Things that would be worth a lot of money if they got out. And not the usual bullshit, the "Taylor is fucking Naomi Campbell" shit. I could put a lot of people in jail ... Think I'm bluffing? Try me ... I dare you ... I ... I miss my angels. I just want to talk to them. To tell them Mommy loves them ... to ... tell them ... I could fucking kill Gary with my bare hands and not blink. I could stare into his eyes as he begged for my mercy and forgiveness and I could snuff out his life and then go back to my lunch as though nothing happened.

I miss them so much. Do they care? Of course not. Hey, some crude garage mix of the little bastards rehearsing Christmas music just went to No. 1 on the Holiday Charts. Think Kenny G is choking on his own cock over that one? I believe these tiny ingrates, who I gave life to, could sing into a bag of their own shit and ten million girls whose life ambition is to someday get breast implants would spend their hard-earned abortion money just to cradle it in their arms.

But hey! It was a great run, huh? Better to burn out than fade away! What do I care? I still have more money than any of you will ever have in a lifetime of being paid by the government not to grow corn.

Merry Fucking Christmas,
God is dead,
Eileen Hanson

LACK OF POWER: THE FORD TAPES

THE FOLLOWING CONVERSATIONS were transcribed from tapes made during the presidential administration of Gerald R. Ford. The tapes were recorded on a voice-activated taping system first installed in the White House Oval Office in 1971 by Richard Nixon, to preserve his administration for historical purposes. Nixon would, in later years, refer to the move as "a huge fuckup." The Ford tapes are permanently housed at the Gerald R. Ford Presidential Foundation and Archives, known colloquially as his son Jack's garage. They are in the box next to the pan of used motor oil. While a majority of the collection has since been taped over with Grateful Dead bootlegs, the remaining tapes offer great insight into the almost two and a half years our thirty-eighth president spent in office.

Historians remain mixed in their judgment of Ford's

presidency, some not remembering that Ford was ever president, others saying, "The guy who makes the cars?" Although this dispute may never be settled, Gerald R. Ford remains the only living president to appear in Disneyland's Hall of Presidents, as himself. Four days a week, two shows a day, with three weeks off in winter, or as it is sometimes known, "the slow season."

CAST OF CHARACTERS

Gerald R. Ford
President

Betty Ford
First Lady

Leonid Brezhnev
Russian Premier

Dick Cheney
Ford Chief of Staff

Al Haig
*Nixon Chief of
Staff*

Jack Hushen
Press Secretary

Henry Kissinger
Secretary of State

Nelson Rockefeller
Vice President

Donald Rumsfeld
Secretary of Defense

Javier Sanchez
Steward

AUGUST 10, 1974: The President, Javier Sanchez
10:12–10:37 A.M., OVAL OFFICE

Newly sworn-in President Ford has been president for less than a day. A nation looks to Ford to restore the dignity and honor of a tarnished office. Javier Sanchez, a White House steward for twenty-three years, shares a moment with the new president on this very difficult day.

(*There are rustling noises, as though searching for something.*)

FORD: Oh, Miss July... I know the old man keeps you in here somewhere... Pretty, pretty Miss July...

(*A door opens.*)

SANCHEZ: Oh... I'm sorry, sir. I didn't know you—

(*A drawer slams shut.*)

FORD: No, No. Sanchez, please come in. I was just... you know there's never a stapler when you... Oh... (*laughs*) here it is... damn stapler. Gotta staple some... staplings.

SANCHEZ: Yes, Mr. President...

FORD: No, no, no. Mr. President must never know I was in here. Is that clear? (*There is a pause.*) No tellie Nixon. (*Louder*) NO TELLIE EL PRESIDENTE... COMPRENDE? Ten dollars for Sanchez. No tellie Presidente.

SANCHEZ: Okay, sir.

FORD: Good, Sanchez... very bien.

SANCHEZ: But you're the president now.

FORD: Yes, yes (*laughs*). Yes, Sanchez. (*Slowly*) I'm— the—President—and—Mr.—Nixon—can—never— know—I—was—in—here. Okay? Ten dollars. Sanchez good. Ford good. Nixon bad... Nixon mean.

SANCHEZ: President Nixon resigned two days ago, sir. You were sworn in as president yesterday.

FORD: That's impossible, Sanchez. I just saw Nixon two days ago and if he resigned who's the Pres—Wait a minute. Yesterday...the party. With that nice man in the black robe.

SANCHEZ: Chief Justice Burger. He swore you in.

FORD: Well, I'll be a sonofabitch. So *that's* why we had that yummy cake. I thought it might have been my birthday, but that was in 1913. So, I'm the president...

(*There is a long silence, followed by snoring.*)

SEPTEMBER 15, 1979: The President, Al Haig, Henry Kissinger
2:34–2:36 P.M., OVAL OFFICE

The two remaining White House employees who still support the previous administration, Haig and Kissinger, fight to convince Ford to sign a full pardon for Nixon and begin the healing process over Watergate.

(*The rustling of paper.*)

FORD: (*laughs*) Oh, Charlie Brown...When will you learn?

(*A door opens.*)

KISSINGER: Good afternoon, Mr. President.

FORD: Hey, Mr. Kissinger. Mr. Haig. Good morning. C'mon in. How are you? Want some juice? (*A glass breaks.*) Damnit.

HAIG: Mr. President, would you sign this please?

(*Papers rustling, followed by a short silence.*)

FORD: I can't sign this.

KISSINGER: I told you, Al. He—

HAIG: Mr. President, the nation needs—

FORD: I don't have a pen...I had one, but Betty took it away. Did you know that pens fit almost perfectly in your eye?

KISSINGER: You can use my pen.

FORD: Seriously? (*whistles*) That's a beauty. What kind of pen is that?

KISSINGER: Um, I believe it is a Cross pen.

FORD: It looks like it's made of gold. They must pay you a pretty penny where you work if you can afford a pen made of gold.

KISSINGER: I think it's gold-plated.

HAIG: Mr. President, if you could just sign on this line.

(*Long silence.*)

FORD: This sure is some pen.

(*Long silence.*)

HAIG: Let him have the pen, Hank.

KISSINGER: But...

FORD: You don't need it? I mean I love the pen, but if, you know, you need it, well...

HAIG: Hank...

KISSINGER: Oh, all right. Mr. President, would you like to keep the pen?

FORD: Are you serious? Wow. That's super. I really—I don't know what to say. This is some beauty.

HAIG: Mr. President?

FORD: Right, right. This paper?

HAIG: Yes.

FORD: Okay. Here we go. Signing my name. Here we go... (*Silence.*) Um, could you hand me that thing?

KISSINGER: What?

FORD: The nameplate. The long thingie sitting on the front of the desk.

HAIG: This?

FORD: Does it have my name on it?

HAIG: Yes.

FORD: That's the one. Thank you. Okay. Here we go. Capital G, little *e*, it's okay if I print, right?

HAIG: Fine.

FORD: Man, this baby handles like a dream (*unintelligible*). Did you know both my names end in *d*?

HAIG: I did not, but thank you, sir. (*Papers rustling.*) Good day.

FORD: No, thank you.

KISSINGER: (*quietly*) Al, you had no right giving him . . .

(*A door closes.*)

FORD: Suckers. This little golden beauty . . . Ahhhhh! My eye!

MAY 12, 1975: The President

The USS *Mayagüez* has been captured in international waters by the Cambodian government. There has been no contact with the ship since its Mayday signal and the fate of the crew rests solely on the shoulders of our thirty-eighth president. Here Gerald R. Ford ponders, in solitude, the drama that is before him.

SEGMENT ONE
8:11 A.M.–12:47 P.M., OVAL OFFICE

FORD: (*Grunting noises.*) C'mon . . . C'mon. (*More grunting.*) Sonofabitch. Think you're tough huh? (*Banging noises, followed by a crash.*) Damnit. (*Grunting noises.*) What the . . . (*Grunting noises.*) C'mon. (*More grunting, doors slamming repeatedly, followed by banging, a very long silence.*) C'mon. (*Heavy breathing, long silence.*)

SEGMENT TWO
12:47–6:23 P.M., OVAL OFFICE

FORD: (*Grunting noises.*) C'mon . . . C'mon. (*Long silence.*) DAMN YOU! (*More grunting.*) Bastard. (*Footsteps walking, getting softer.*) All right, let's see what you got. (*Footsteps running, getting louder, then a crash.*) Goddamnit. You sonofa— (*More grunting, then fast banging.*) Please! . . . So . . . tired . . .

(*A door opens.*)

BETTY FORD: Jerry?

FORD: Oh, Betty. Thank God you're awake. Can you open this?

BETTY FORD: The Coke? Sure, Toots. (*Cracking sound.*)

FORD: Oh my God! Didn't that hurt your mouth?

BETTY FORD: Not a problem, sailor.

FORD: (*Gurgling and slurping.*) So . . . thirsty.

JULY 21, 1975: The President, Leonid Brezhnev
1:33–1:42 P.M., WHITE HOUSE RED PHONE

President Ford attempts to follow up on the historic July 19, 1975, linking up of the American spacecraft *Apollo* and the Russian craft *Soyuz*. The mission presents a critical window of diplomatic opportunity for the two opposing world leaders. It also represents the first time Ford seems aware of the taping system.

(*Phone rings . . . and rings. Short silence. Phone rings again.*)

FORD: What? (*Phone continues to ring.*) Hello? Who's there? Is this some kind of a joke?

(*An object is put down. Phone continues to ring.*) Oh! Hello?

BREZHNEV: Hello, Mr. President.

FORD: Mr. Kissinger, is that you?

BREZHNEV: No. It's . . .

FORD: You sound just like Mr. Kissinger.

BREZHNEV: It's Chairman Brezhnev.

FORD: Who?

BREZHNEV: Brezhnev.

FORD: All right . . .

(*Long silence.*)

BREZHNEV: And uh . . . I want to congratulate our countries' successful space mission of détente. It is a great step toward ending this cold war. (*Long silence.*) And . . . uh . . . well, I just wanted to say if cooperation between our nations brings such—

FORD: (*Panel being opened.*) What the hell is . . . ?

BREZHNEV: Excuse me?

FORD: What are these buttons? (*A button being pressed. The sound of rewinding, another button press.*) *"What are these buttons?"* Holy shit! That's *my* voice!

BREZHNEV: May I inquire what is—

FORD: I'm sorry, Mr. Kissinger. I'm gonna have to call you later. (*A phone hanging up, followed by buttons and rewinding.*) *"Holy Shit! That's my voice."* (*laughs*) My name is Gerald Ford. (*Buttons rewinding.*) *". . . call you later. My name is Gerald Ford."* (*Laughs, a loud belch, buttons, rewinding.*) *". . . Ford. (Belch.)"* (*Laughs, buttons rewinding.*) *"(Belch)."* (*Long laughter.*) AND NOW, AT QUARTERBACK, A SIX FOOT ONE INCH SOPHOMORE FROM MICHIGAN . . . GERALD FORD! (*Loud belch, buttons, rewinding.*) *". . . SOPHOMORE FROM MICHIGAN . . . GERALD FORD! (Loud belch)"* (*Laughs, singing.*) You can tell by the way I use my walk, I'm a ladies' man, no rhyme or chalk. (*Buttons, rewinding, buttons.*) *". . . man, no rhyme or chalk."* (*Laughs.*)

OCTOBER 1, 1976: The President, Dick Cheney, Jack Hushen, Nelson Rockefeller, Donald Rumsfeld 9:15–11:30 A.M., OVAL OFFICE

The president, with the consultation of his cabinet, discusses strategy for the upcoming debate with Democratic nominee Jimmy Carter. All points of view must be faithfully weighed to assure the proper strategy.

CHENEY: Perhaps if we were to take focus away from the inflation issue ...

HUSHEN: For Christ sake, Dick, how? Those guys are gonna hammer us on the economy, we know that.

RUMSFELD: Look, Carter's a governor. He's vulnerable on foreign policy. I say we play that as our trump and—

ROCKEFELLER: We could rehash the Bicentennial and Olympics shit.

HUSHEN: Bingo. Go blatant sentimentality. America and apple pie. Pride and—

FORD: Fellas?

CHENEY: Yes, Mr. President?

FORD: Has anyone seen my hat?

(*Long silence.*)

HUSHEN: Um. You mean the one on your head?

FORD: Huh? I ... Well ... No. The one with the picture of the bear on ... Arggghh. Ma ... Chhhhh.

CHENEY: Christ, he's swallowing the—

HUSHEN: He's choking, someone help me here. Grab the brim before—

FORD: CHHHHHHH!

JANUARY 21, 1977: The President, Javier Sanchez
11:11–11:15 A.M. OVAL OFFICE

A subdued Gerald Ford bids farewell to his faithful
and trusted staff before reentering private life. The elec-
tion of 1976 was hard fought, but in the end President
Ford could not overcome the stigma associated with
the Republican Party after Watergate. He had served
the office with honor, and could exit the presidency
with dignity. The completion of a long journey . . . an
arduous task completed, a new challenge awaiting.

(*A television plays a tennis match in the background. A door opens.*)

SANCHEZ: Oh . . . I'm sorry, sir, I didn't realize you were
still—

FORD: Ah, Sanchez my man. Entrez vous. You ever see
this Renee Richards play tennis? Hot-cha-cha. (*A growl-
ing noise, like a tiger.*)

SANCHEZ: Uh . . . sir?

FORD: Hey, Sanchez, we got any more of that yummy
dessert from yesterday?

SANCHEZ: The Carter Inaugural Cake?

FORD: Is that what it's called? Man oh man that was
good eating. For a second I thought it was my birthday,
but that was in 1913.

MARTHA STEWART'S VAGINA

THE PARTY WAS a smashing success. Your handmade bees-wax candles (*Martha Stewart Living*, September 1996) cast a hypnotic spell on the veranda. Your sausage profiteroles (Dec. '96) moistened the mouths of every male within fifty feet of the buffet steam table you constructed out of lemon rinds and old LPs (May '95). Now it's time to relax, let down your hair, open a bottle of Grand Marnier, and select one of the illegal alien bartenders you hired for some all-night fun (April '97, "Having Sex with the Help"). You've earned it. But something is not quite right. You spent so much time being a hostess you forgot to be a woman. And now the time is right for making love, but your vagina is a mess. I've been there ... and it's not a good thing. You have got to remember Party Rule #1: There is no party as important as the party you're about to throw in your vagina.

No area of home entertaining remains as exciting or ignored as the vagina. A recent letter from one of my readers is a typical example.

Dear Martha,

I'm from Los Gatos, New Mexico, and I loved your new book How to Decorate. *So much of the book is devoted to wall coverings and tapestries, but I wonder if more time could be given to the art of marbling a finish.*

A big fan,
Felice Damper

P.S. My vagina is a mess.

I hear you. So many of my women friends have developed incredibly sophisticated taste when it comes to throwing the perfect theme party or just relaxing at home in their newly refurbished den. Their sense of style has grown and flourished as they have, yet their most cherished spot has gone unchanged. Throw rugs and Ikea lamps were fine in college, but you're a woman now.

EXTERIORS

It's not just about hygiene, it's about first impressions . . . Don't get caught with your pants down!

Although lovemaking is a scheduled activity, most of us don't use the weeks of downtime effectively, and before you know it, it's the third Tuesday of the month, and he can't wait for you to primp. That's why I prefer a method of maintenance that requires less constant vigilance. You may find that it even allows for a little spontaneity. I have several ways of dealing with this age-old problem.

First: Hair is unruly. Get rid of it.

Second: The area is cleared, but remember, the exterior is your first chance to make an impression on a prospective lover. You must make the space look warm and inviting, but also exclusive. The outside of your vagina must say, "Enjoy!! But understand you're lucky to be here!!"

An undressed vagina can make a bold statement, but if you're like me you probably want something a bit more dignified and versatile. Most vagina treatments derive their character from the fabric. Cotton says you're ready Freddie, velvet says enjoy the luxury (and it's a wonderful buffer against chafing), and silk says you do a lot of dry cleaning. In any event, guard against heavy draping and intricate patterns. One, because it traps dirt, and two, because you don't want him to be distracted. Remember, the easier and cleaner the design, the less time he'll spend admiring and the more time he'll spend enjoying.

I was once dating a well-heeled museum curator. I made a vagina treatment out of a miniaturized Monet. The facade looked wonderful from a distance, but once my lover got up close he said it just looked like a bunch of colored dots. We spent the next two hours arguing the merits of Pointillism and Renaissance realism. The mood was broken.

If you're promiscuous you may want a more basic, non-individualized approach. Nothing is more embarrassing than a personalized vagina treatment that's been personalized for someone else. Years ago I was engaged in an unrepentant affair with a member of the Irish Liberation Movement, Sinn Fein. My vagina treatment at the time was linen with pressed four-leaf clovers and the simple inscription: FREE IRELAND. The linen's cool summer comfort caused me to forget I had it on while hosting a very elegant lawn party. Later that night I found myself in an amorous embrace with one of my distinguished guests. Needless to say this blood relative of Winston Churchill was not amused.

Not all vagina treatments require that kind of intricate detailing or creativity. For the summer you may want to go with simple horizontal pull shades or a top-hanging translucent white cotton drape. One you can easily pull aside for a dramatic voilà effect. Again, don't get too complicated with pulleys, rods and weights. The vagina treatment must be easily operated. Nothing invites impotence like agitation. A translucent white cotton drape is elegant and dramatic and the perfect summertime statement. It hangs from a simple bamboo rod suspended just below the navel. Closed, it gives the ambience of the windswept beaches of Nantucket. Open, it says, "I'm making love on the cabana porch with a Caribbean island native who I literally met ten minutes ago, while my jackass husband searches in vain for a golf course."

INTERIOR

Two lips and a clitoris do not a vagina make.

Basic anatomy may be crucial to certain biological func-
tions, but we ask more from our vaginas than almost any
other area of our bodies or houses. Phillip Abercrombie
outlines these expectations in *The Philosophy of Interior Vaginal
Design*: "To let in air but keep out rain, to allow view but
maintain privacy, to let in the penis without cold, dust,
noise, friction or excessive heat, and to vary at will the
amounts of all these substances." A heady task for a complex area.

First, we must undertake to determine the actual usage.
It has been my experience that most women vastly underuse
their vaginas, thinking of it only occasionally for sex or
hygiene. This is shortsighted. Think of it as nature's spare
room, a multifaceted everyspace. We all know of its in-
herent sexual design, but did you know that some vaginas
are used as temporary housing? People have actually been
known to live in a vagina for up to nine months. Uninvited
guests can be a real challenge to the unprepared host. Don't
get caught short.

It doesn't stop there. I have a friend who lost her ocean-
side office space during Hurricane Andrew. Her business,
a vanity boutique supported by a rich paramour, didn't
qualify for disaster relief. It seemed she was out of luck
and out of work. Not so. A little ingenuity and some good
old-fashioned MS know-how had my friend back on her

feet in no time. She has been happily working out of her vagina for eighteen months now and says she'll never go back to a conventional space. The convenience and security a vaginal office provides more than make up for the occasional awkwardness and minor discomfort of answering the phone. Not to mention it's a nifty tax write-off.

Here are some interiors that I have experimented with in the past. All three will provide for a more versatile and productive vagina.

THE VAGINAL OFFICE: Cupboards built into the wall provide efficiency and convenience. Phone, fax and computer on sliding trays give access to whatever you're using and can hide away for holiday office parties. The lamp is a floor model to provide maximum reading potential.

PRIVATE MOMENTS: Your vagina can be a place of serenity and introspection. A porch swing suspended by birch branches provides a welcome respite from daily travails. A ceiling fan gives cool relief in any season and some Parisian folding chairs (cushions slip over the back and tie down) are weatherproofed for unexpected company.

SEX: The sex vagina is sparse but not cold. Few furnishings leave wonderfully open space, plenty of room for strenuous decadence. Strong horizontal lines on a rattan throw rug give a lived-in, spontaneous air. Some simple floor lighting is a real space saver and sets a spectacularly romantic mood. Install a Murphy bed. They fold down for unexpected use. Accidents do happen and an actual human being may need to bunk here for upwards of nine months. The Murphy bed says you're ready for anything. (In the case of multiple guests I recommend Vaginal Trundle Beds. Comfort and storage during the day.)

THE THING TO REMEMBER: Although the vagina is not on public display, it can still be the centerpiece of your personal style. Use it wisely. Whether you're dealing with exterior treatments or interior furnishings, allow comfort to inspire and utility to inform . . . and don't skimp. It's your vagina, and you get only one. Follow my simple instructions: you will never again have the unsettling fear that your guests will know that underneath those sparkling Harry Winston earrings and formfitting Christian Dior gown lies a vagina from Filene's Basement.

THE NEW JUDAISM

THERE IS NO doubt Judaism in America has reached an important crossroads. The figures are astonishing. Fifty percent of all currently single American Jews will intermarry, 10 percent will convert to another religion and half of the remaining 40 percent will help them convert or intermarry by watching their dogs. The Rabbinical Congress has estimated that by the year 2010, Jewish life in America will have deteriorated to the point where a *Seinfeld* reunion special will be a non-sweeps event, perhaps even buried in summer reruns. The certainty of this apocalyptic prediction was hotly contested by a small but vocal contingent of rabbis. They threatened to walk out of the proceedings unless the suffix *ish* was added to the predicted year 2010. Rabbi Tarfon punctuated the debate by shouting, "I mean, can we really be sure about the year?" before disrobing and setting fire to his caftan. Rabbi Benjamin Rosenzweig then sparked a near riot from the Orthodox contingent with his barbed query "if 'ish,' why not 'or so'?" while Rabbis Eliezer and Johnson exchanged blows over whether or not Fruit Smoothies were kosher. Calm was restored only after the elders' promise of a fall seminar on the grooming of long beards.

Cause for alarm? Judaism has a long and storied history of surviving threats of extinction.

THE SPANISH INQUISITION

In 1492, led by Ferdinand and Isabella, the Christians conquered the last of then Muslim Spain. They immediately decreed all Jews must convert to Christianity or be expelled. Many Jews left. Many Jews, however, had already put money down for time-share condos in Majorca, and had no choice but to convert or lose their deposit. Those Jews who stayed in Spain converted to Christianity, only to be systematically hunted down during the Inquisition, accused of heresy against the church for being Jews. This prompted a direct descendant of the great Jewish intellectual Maimonides to protest the Inquisition, saying, "Isn't that kind of a catch-22?"

GRAND INQUISITOR'S SOPHISTICATED
METHOD OF INTERROGATION

INQUISITOR: Are you a Jew?

JEW: No.

INQUISITOR: Are you sure you're not a Jew?

JEW: Yes.

INQUISITOR: Oh well, sorry to trouble you. Would you like to stay for cake?

JEW: Is it chocolate? I'm allergic to chocolate.

INQUISITOR: It's an out-of-this-world lemon pound cake.

JEW: Well, maybe just a nosh . . .

The Inquisitor smiles a sinister smile.

JEW: Damn.

THE THIRD REICH

The horrors of the Holocaust are well documented. Adolf Hitler's rise to power remains the greatest obstacle to survival Judaism has yet overcome. Hitler's systematic Final Solution was responsible for the death of six million. He was a monster, although it is said that early in his career he would end a particularly virulent anti-Semitic diatribe with the phrase "no offense." Nazi Germany was so destructive to Judaism not only for the loss of life, but because many who survived began to view the practice of Judaism as somewhat of a health hazard.

THE BURGER KING BACON, EGG AND CHEESE
CROISSAN'WICH

A sinful combination of pork, cheese and egg. The Triple Crown of nonkosher living—why does it have to be so delicious?

•   •   •

Judaism has shown remarkable resilience in the face of great external threat. But these threats have been nearly eliminated in America. Total assimilation is the new threat to American Judaism and is more sinister because it goes to the core problem. Judaism is no longer able to compete in a free market religious environment. Although *pizzazz* sounds like it could be a Yiddish word, it's something Judaism is sorely lacking. We must present a new Judaism. To understand what is necessary, we must first understand the fundamentals as they exist now.

Modern American Judaism can be broken down into three simple categories.

ORTHODOX

Orthodox Jews, or, as they are known in the Talmud, the Really Chosen Ones, are committed to the idea that the entire Torah was dictated by God verbatim to Moses at Mount Sinai. Therefore all the original Torah's laws must be obeyed as written. Other forms of Judaism dispute this claim, although it does explain certain passages in the first Torah, such as "I'm sorry, am I boring you?" and "What do you like better, Moses, Lord Almighty or Big Hoohah?" Orthodox Jews observe a strict Sabbath, the separation of sexes during worship and believe Jackie Mason is the funniest man alive. They are also rumored to engage in sex only through a hole in their bedsheets, a falsehood that spread after a particularly wild Halloween party at the Mendelsohns'.

CONSERVATIVE

Conservative Jews are Orthodox Jews who went coed, reportedly after one of their more influential members attended a mixer at Barnard. They generally believe the Torah was passed down from God to Moses, but was edited or at least spell-checked first. The main difference between Conservative and Orthodox Jews is summed up beautifully in Conservative Rabbi Mishner's seminal work titled *Hey Fellas, How 'Bout We Take It Down a Notch?* Conservatives believe Woody Allen is the funniest man alive.

REFORM

Reform Jews are the children of Conservative Jews, or as they are sometimes known, Christians with curlier hair. They believe the Torah is very long and hard to read because it's written in a foreign language. They are not required to adhere to any strict religious doctrine but are still able to take off work on at least 75 percent of all Jewish Holidays. They believe Carrot Top is the funniest man alive.

A COMPARATIVE CHART

	ORTHODOX	CONSERVATIVE	REFORM
DREAM JOB	Rabbi	Doctor	VJ
DIETARY CODE	Strict Kosher	Zabar's	Liposuction
MUSIC	Klezmer	Streisand	Gospel
MOVIE	*Shoah*	*Schindler's List*	Anything with Steve Guttenberg
DREAM WIFE	Mom	Amy Irving	Kate Capshaw
SABBATH	A day of worship	A day of reflection	Saturday
FAVORITE BALL-PLAYER	Hank Greenberg	Sandy Koufax	Ken Griffey, Jr.
HOMOSEXUALITY	A sin	A sin . . . but oh, what they've done for Broadway theater	Something that happened at camp
GUILT	Total	Total	Total

No present form of American Judaism currently has the appeal to sustain us as a people through the next millennium. A new Judaism must be created to battle the erosion of our population caused by defection, apathy and blondes. If we don't watch out, the Hare Krishnas will soon be kicking our ass.

SOLUTION

The Children. There is a fable in Deuteronomy: A poor farmer from the Tribe of Levi came one day to King Solomon, the wisest of kings and the only one who could juggle. The farmer begged Solomon for his wisdom. "My only son has lost a baby tooth. All day and night he cries for reparation. He suffers loudly...even the cattle have complained." Solomon looked up from his crossword puzzle, pondered the farmer's dilemma and spoke. "Cut this child in half. Each family can have one half. This will end the dispute." The farmer looked stricken. "Gotcha!" said Solomon. "I'm sorry, sometimes I can't help myself." The farmer sighed. "How old's the boy?" asked Solomon. "Four plantings and half a harvest," replied the farmer. "Okay, here's what you do," continued the wise king, "Tell the boy to put the tooth under his pillow tonight. When he sleeps, replace the tooth with a piece of candy or a quarter. Tell him the...I don't know, the Angel of Teeth came down to reclaim his property. This will solve your problem." "Who would believe that?" the farmer asked skeptically. "What is lightning?" asked Solomon. "God testing batteries," the farmer replied. Solomon looked at the farmer knowingly. "Oh...I see what you mean," said the farmer. Solomon smiled, "Want to see me juggle two olives and a pomegranate?"

What is the point? People will believe anything if you catch them early enough.

OUR GOD

The Jewish concept of God is too difficult to fathom. An omniscient, omnipotent Peeping Tom who loves us and smites our enemies. Although recent history suggests he's a little slow on the smiting. We were created in his image, but you can't see him or describe him. And why did he give us so much back hair?

The Christians had it right. Want to worship Jesus? Here's a picture of him on the wall next to the refrigerator. There's even one on black velvet. Not enough? Look at these movies he did. Long hair, sad eyes, trim . . . not a bad-looking fellow. Put him on your dashboard and go! He's even got his own musicals. As Nietzsche wrote, "God is dead. But he lives on at the Brooks Atkinson Theater in a spectacular revival of *Godspell.*"

If Judaism wants to compete, we need to personify our vision of God. In the new Judaism, God will now be referred to as Uncle Pete. A friendly gentleman in his forties, Uncle Pete is still all-powerful but he's also tangible. He's about five feet ten, although his license says six feet, 170 pounds, and smells like a freshly baked pie. Wondering how God could let children die? Well, let's get ol' Uncle Pete in here and find out. I'm sure he has a reasonable explanation!

OUR HISTORY

The history of the Jewish people has been described in many scholarly manuscripts as "the shit end of the stick." Even the recently translated Dead Sea Scrolls end with the phrase "Watch your back." The threat of persecution has not been offset by the promise of an occasional nice brisket. The New Judaism will deemphasize historical trouble for a more positive outlook. Up to now being the Chosen Ones has brought nothing but trouble. In the New Judaism, all Chosen Ones will receive a value pack worth hundreds of dollars in discounts at participating vendors (for example, 10 percent off any dinner at Friendly's, with purchase of a Fishamajig sandwich).

OLD JUDAISM PASSOVER SEDER

CHILD: Why on this night do we eat bitter herbs?

ADULT: To remind us of the pain our ancestors felt while enslaved in Egypt.

NEW JUDAISM PASSOVER SEDER

CHILD: Why on this night do we eat hot fudge sundaes?

ADULT: To remind us that being Jewish is like having your birthday every day!! Plus they're delicious!

OUR LAWS

The key word here is *simplify*. The Torah and Old Testament are all over the place. Thou shalt not kill. Thou shalt not commit adultery. Don't eat pork. Not only do some rules seem arbitrary, the language is very B.C. The New Judaism simplifies the rules of conduct into a concise, hip jargon the young people will really go for. The new rules are: Ass, gas or grass, nobody rides for free; and Be cool.

OUR MASCOT

"Jews have a mascot?" you ask. No. This is a problem. Any new idea that expects to have legs in the marketplace needs a lovable mascot to represent and brand the product with the populace. Just ask Santa. How many Jews have felt the pain of trying to compete during the Christmas season by concocting a mascot, the personification of their own gift-giving holiday? A Hanukkah Harry, the swarthy man in charge of Jewish kids' presents who waits until the Christmas rush has ended to try and get some decent bargains, only to find the good toys gone. The New Judaism takes a page from the playbook of successful ventures like Christianity and R. J. Reynolds with the unveiling of our new character, Jewey. Jewey's a cool, camel-like character (actually Joe Camel with some slight retooling) who brings laughter and joy to all the Kinder. Imagine a Bar Mitzvah boy's excitement at knowing he just became a man, and that Jewey's on his way with money and cigarettes. And here's the best part ... He can fly!!

CONCLUSION

As Karl Marx wrote, "Religion is the opiate of the people, and who couldn't use a little opiate every now and again." People want religion. They like it. It makes them feel secure and confident in a world of uncertainty, besides giving them a place to go on weekends. You just have to make sure your religion is appealing enough. If we are to reduce Portnoy's Complaint to a suggestion, we must leave behind the bounds of the Old Judaism and retool. The New Judaism will ensure the continuation and flourishing of the Jewish people well into the twenty-first century. Mazel Tov and All Praise to Uncle Pete.

PEN PALS

October 3, 1994

Dear Mother Teresa,

Hi. You don't know me but my name is Diana and I'm your biggest fan. I've never written a letter like this before so don't think I'm crazy but I think you're the coolest. The more I hear about you the more I think we're like sisters or something, where one of the sisters is this really beautiful princess and the other isn't.

I want to know everything about you. Where do you live? I know you spend a lot of time in India, which is really weird because I live in England and India used to be one of our colonies. Do you spend summers there? I hear it's really hot. Do you drink tea? Iced tea? Have you ever been to Monaco? It's totally fun.

I'm married, are you? You're probably too busy what with the lepers and everything. I think it's kind of fun to be married. Well I guess I should be going, Cindy Crawford is coming to meet my kids and then we have to go to an Elton John concert—yuccck! Anyway, I would love to meet you for a drink or coffee, whatever, my treat! Please write back or call me soon. You can call collect (but don't make it a habit ... ha-ha).

Your friend (hopefully),
Her Royal Highness
Diana
Princess of Wales
Buckingham Palace
Suite #3
London, England

P.S. I'm not crazy.

November 12, 1994

Dear Mother of All Big Snobs,

Braaaaaay!! Braaaaaaay!! Do you know what that sound is? It's the sound an ass makes, which is what I feel like after writing you with an offer of friendship and never hearing back. I really thought you were different but I guess you're just too big and important to write. I could have any friend I want including any of the surviving Beatles and I chose you. But I guess that doesn't matter to a bigshot like you huh?

Maybe all those people on TV who say such nice things about you don't really know you or maybe if I had some stupid disease like leprosy or hemophilia you'd find it in your supposedly big heart to answer my letter. I hate you. Actually I don't even care enough to hate you. You could row to England, then walk to London, then crawl to the palace and beg me to be your friend and I wouldn't. I have a good mind to tell my husband THE FUTURE KING about this but I'm afraid he would bomb you and your stupid country bumpkin charity house.

Your ex-friend,
Princess Diana
London, England

P.S. Some people pay up to 100,000 pounds for a simple picture of me in my workout tights. Beat that!!!

November 11, 1994

Dear Supporter,

Thank you for your interest in Mother Teresa's Charities of Hope foundation. As you know the Living Saint's schedule is quite busy so we will not be able to schedule the requested meeting.

The Charities of Hope foundation provides for the basic care of thousands of indigents in the Calcutta region. We have enclosed literature concerning the good works of the Living Saint and the Charities of Hope foundation. We very much appreciate any support you can give.

God bless you,
Sisters of Charity
Charities of Hope
Calcutta, India

November 14, 1994

Dearest friend Mother Teresa,

I just got your letter and I am soooo sorry for the terrible things I said to you in my last letter which you probably just got. I forgot how very slow the mail is in Third World regions. Please, please, please forgive me. I beg forgiveness even though friends like us don't usually have to do that, it's just understood.

I know this sounds crazy but I feel like we've known each other for years or in another lifetime or something. Like I was this beautiful Egyptian princess and you were my super great Egyptian servant/friend who I could confide in. I've enclosed a picture of myself (I'm the one standing in the carriage!). I know I look so fat but I don't care. The pale man with the big ears to my right is my husband, Prince Charles (Charles the turd I call him). Does he seem dull and devoid of any passion in the picture? He is in real life. I've had more passionate evenings with the Energizer Bunny if you know what I mean!! Normally I would be clearer with what I mean but I'm not because friends like us have an unspoken bond of understanding that means I don't have to be clear or specific.

Please send me a picture of yourself and I will put it on one of my dressers in one of the houses I use more frequently than the other ones.

Thank you in advance,
Your Dear Soulmate,
Diana
England

P.S. Sometimes I want to kill myself.

January 4, 1995

Dear Mr. (Miss) Mrs. Diana,

Thank you for your interest in Mother Teresa. We regret that we do not send pictures of the Living Saint to her admirers. We have enclosed literature on Mother Teresa's Charities of Hope foundation. Thank you again for your interest.

Sisters of Charity
Charities of Hope
Calcutta

ONE YEAR LATER

January 10, 1996

Hey Girlfriend,

I know it's been a week since my last letter but things have been crazy here. Miss me? Anyway I'll get right to the point. Free at last, free at last. Thank God Almighty... Free at last!!! The divorce came through days ago and I couldn't be more pleased. Well... I'm 25 million pounds pleased at least. By the way, how many Royals does it take to screw in a lightbulb?... Give up?... nine!! Prince William to screw it in and the other eight to go fuck themselves.

Your guidance has meant so much to me. I couldn't have had the strength without you. I feel reborn. I've been a Lady so long I've forgotten how to be a woman... (not counting the rugby squad I wrote about in my letters of July 17–21).

How are you? How's that thing going in India? Any new men? You're so pretty but you always play it down. I wish you'd let me make you over as I requested in my letters of May 12, 1994, August 5, 1994, and March 22, 1995. Now that I'm single again I'm not taking no for an answer. Some of my lesser girlfriends and I are discussing plans for an all-girls Mexican Fiesta in Cabo. If I'm not mistaken there's a margarita there with your name on it.

By the way you never answered my question of June 19, 1995—salt or no salt?

Missing you terribly,
Di-Di
Kensington Palace
England

P.S. What has sixteen legs, inbred genetic defects and a giant stick up its ass? Give up?!... The Royal Family!!!!!

August 11, 1997

Hey You,

    You little scamp!! I hadn't heard from you in ages and I thought maybe you hadn't liked the matching swimsuits I had made for us... and I was actually quite upset about it, until watching the telly one day I find out you've been in hospital. Do you think so little of me that you didn't want to burden me with your troubles? After all we've been through? Well, I've enclosed a get well card, including a bit of philosophy concerning friendship. I don't want to give it away but it's a drawing of two naked imps holding hands with the caption "Friendship is being there for the tough times." I believe this has been the credo for our relationship and have personalized the imps by hand to drive the point home. (I'm the imp with the full chest and you're the one with wrinkles.) I only hope you take this message to heart as I am quite disappointed with your lack of candor about your health. I've also included brownies in this care package. You really should be careful of the food down there. After my unfortunate run-in with an intestinal parasite off the coast of Fiji I've learned the value of hygienic food preparation.

On a more upbeat note, I've met someone!! He's rich and dashing and here's the best part...He's a darkie!!! I think you'll agree that forbidden fruit tastes the sweetest...and won't that burn the Queen Mother's Royal Ass!!!

Luv,
D.

P.S. Don't worry about the sex. We're being safe.

October 1, 1997

Dear Earl Charles Spencer,

We were all greatly saddened to hear of Princess Diana's untimely passing. As you begin the processes of healing and determining the Princess's final wishes, please keep in mind the Charities of Hope foundation. We know you have wisely begun a foundation in Diana's name, to continue with her good works. As you may know, our late beloved Mother Teresa and the Princess were great friends and constant correspondents. Perhaps it is fate that we continue, in their absence, the relationship they had so energetically forged. Also, to reassure you, it would be a legal write-off.

God Bless You,
Sisters of Charity
Charities of Hope
Calcutta

LOCAL NEWS

Well-Known Taco Bell Chihuahua Killed in Bar Fight

ANAHEIM (AP): Señor Jangles, the four-legged star of the Taco Bell commercials, died last night following a physical altercation at an adult entertainment establishment in Anaheim. He was forty-nine years old. Jangles, whose real name was Shaky Pete, was beloved by audiences for being a cute dog that could talk. Today, Señor Jangles was described by distraught friends as a fine actor and a good boy.

Jangles broke into acting in 1993 at the age of fourteen when a representative of the William Morris Agency discovered the talented Chihuahua talking to himself on a Los Angeles street corner. Jangles found steady commercial work soon after the fortuitous meeting, and in 1995 the chatty Chihuahua booked the role of Pepe the Mexican Ladle in the animated Disney film *Oh My God, Our Appliances Can Talk!* But it was Jangles's role in the Taco Bell campaign that would bring his greatest notoriety.

Jangles attained great fame and wealth through the Taco Bell campaign, but friends of the star reported he had grown despondent in recent months. Sources close to Jangles claim he began to view his commercial role as degrading and spoke often of what he perceived as Hollywood's closed-mindedness toward Latino actors. Jangles would also speak of the hypocrisy of a society that allowed him to sell food he would never be allowed to eat off the table. The tensions came to a head three weeks ago when Jangles reportedly walked off the set during the filming of a Taco Bell spot after refusing to don a sombrero and serape. Jangles's publicist refused comment but did say Jangles was suffering from hip dysplasia and had been taking prescribed painkillers at the time of the alleged work stoppage.

The alleged incident leading to Jangles's death occurred around one in the morning. Authorities say Jangles had been in the adult establishment drinking for hours and had been repeatedly warned about licking his crotch. Around midnight, James MacPherson, forty-three, entered the bar and soon thereafter became involved in an argument with the four-legged pitchman. While details of the incident are still unclear, Diamond, a dancer at the popular adult nightspot, believes MacPherson, an unemployed long-haul trucker, took offense at comments Jangles made about his tipping. Others report the brouhaha was touched off when

Jangles, hackles raised, pointed at MacPherson and shouted, *"Tu padre tiene mucho pelo en su pinga"* (Your father has a very hairy penis). Witnesses do agree on two points. Only one punch was thrown and Señor Jangles's last words were *"Ay caramba"* (Oy vey).

MacPherson's lawyers denied reports that their client instigated the attack on the popular canine. They insisted that MacPherson acted only in self-defense after an enraged and inebriated Jangles ignored numerous pleas to sit and stay. Tonight MacPherson is in custody awaiting arraignment on second-degree murder charges.

"It's such a shame," said Diamond. "Mr. Jangles told me he was through with Taco Bell and was going to head to New York and Broadway—to play Rizzo in *Grease.* His whole body was shaking and he seemed really excited . . . or cold."

Señor Jangles is survived by his mother, Pretty Peggy, of San Diego. The identity of his father is unknown, and he had no children due to a childhood operation.

THE LAST SUPPER, OR THE DEAD WAITER

THE LACK OF information and interpretation concerning the life and times of Jesus Christ has, for years, frustrated scholars, theologians and lovers of information and interpretation. To date, the only notable published material on the subject is Franz Shecter's thorough yet ambiguous dissertation, "That Guy from the Thing." So little is known of Jesus because, as Shecter asserts, "He died a long time ago."

This virtual blackout has recently been lifted, in light of an astonishing discovery in the Sinai Peninsula. A German tourist in Israel, searching for the keys to his luggage, stumbled upon an ancient city buried beneath two thousand years of desert sand and a Starbucks. A month's excavation later, this man, still wearing the same pants and shirt he originally traveled in, found what is to date the only written account pertaining to the existence of Jesus Christ. The manuscript contains explicit reference to a dinner party Jesus had with twelve male friends. It is an eyewitness account penned by Avram the Waiter, who served the Christ party at the then-popular Jerusalem eatery, Jerry's. The conventional wisdom concerning the manuscript was that it proved Shecter's Crucifixion hypothesis of a "bachelor party gone awry." Although when Schecter reread the document, this time with his glasses on, grave doubts arose. Now you can decide for yourself as the ancient memoir has finally been translated from its original Spanglish.

THE MANUSCRIPT OF "AVRAM THE WAITER"

So much for things being slow during Passover. It was April of 33 and as usual Jerry's was jammed. Jerry's was the "in" spot of the moment. Ever since Pilate started coming here the place has been packed with gawkers and wannabes. Personally, I could care less. You're a person; I'm a person. Doesn't matter if you're Augustus or Barabbas. You treat me with respect, you get good service. Anyway, I'm at the end of an eight-hour double, slopping kishke to drunken centurions, and in walks Jesus with his flock of hangers-on. "Here comes trouble," I say to Moishe the barback. We'd all seen Jesus and his little bunch of frat boys around town and believe me, *not impressed*. The Greeks invented a lot of great things—namely naked wrestling—but fraternities, or any other platonic male organization for that matter, weren't one of them.

So Luke, he's the skinny one with the greasy hair—
oops, that's all of them—Luke says to me with a snotty
attitude, "Table for thirteen . . . I believe it's under *Christ*."
So I check the book. "Well, I can't find your reservation
and besides, it looks like there's only eight of you here," I
say to him. I'm telling him the truth, by the way, not just
being pissy. They didn't have a reservation and even if they
did, I can't seat them if the whole party hasn't shown.
Sorry, but it's not my rule. "They're coming. They'll be
here. They got a little hung up. Holiday traffic," Luke says.
You're kidding! Hung up in traffic? Well, that changes
everything . . . please. Anyway, the guy's just checking out
the scene, not even looking me in the eye. So all I say is,
and Moishe will back me up on this, "You're welcome to
hang out in the bar and wait for them . . . But I'm afraid—"
and boom, he's on me. "Wait in the bar? You want *us* to
wait in the bar. We're not waiting in the bar, little man."
The way he was carrying on you'd have thought I asked
him to bathe. (P.S. If Jesus is right and there is an afterlife,
I hope they've got soap.)

"Let me ask you something. What year is it?" Luke
says. I know what he's going for but I play dumb. "What
do you mean?" I ask innocently. You should have seen me,
all wide-eyed and sheepish. Elijah caught my performance
and said he was going to throw me a graduation party
because it was obvious I no longer needed acting classes.
"33 *A.D.*," Luke says. I just let it hang there. "*Anno Domini?*
. . . Year of *the Lord*," he says, giving the head nod over in
Christ's direction. "You got me?" he says. So I turn to him
real cool and go, "Well last time *I* checked *my* calendar

it was still 3706." And then I snap my fingers and go back to marrying ketchups. Luke's jaw about hit the floor. Moishe turns and says, "Bathsheba one, Luke zero." It was really funny, but I wasn't just being a bitch. A lot of the folks at Jerry's did still use the Hebrew calendar. And besides, with that attitude those boys weren't getting any special treatment from me. Jesus slips his tunic over his head just like the rest of us; I don't care who his father is.

I do have to admit I was a little scared. Some of these apostles are pretty rough trade, the blue-collar Nazareth crowd. And I think the others work out. They were pissed. Luke was yelling at me, saying if they don't get their table right away, Jesus is going to turn all our Château Lafite-Rothschild into low-grade zinfandel. "Do it!" I say. It's not like it's my wine.

Jesus' boys are in a bit of a frenzy, giving me the third degree. "What's your name?" "We want to talk to the manager!" "Fine," I say, "talk to the manager. Get me fired." I'm an artisan/poet. I'm putting up a night of spoken word in three weeks. I don't need to take shit from cult members. I should have gotten the Etruscan bouncer, Vito the Unreasonable. He'd have thrown them out on their apostles. So just as I'm about to hurl some sea salt in Peter's face, Jesus pipes up. "Boys," he says. "Please. The wise builder doesn't build on sand, but the foolish builder can't build on rock." I had no idea what he was talking about, but suddenly, the angry mob's all kittens and puppies. It's "Right, Rabbi." "Sorry, Rabbi." "Couldn't have put it better myself, Teacher." Please! They're so affected. Jesus could've said, "Hey, look at me, I've got a banana up my ass!" and they would've acted like they just heard the word of God.

Finally, everybody shows up. It's nine o'clock. It's my last table, and the kitchen wants to close. So lucky me has to try and wrangle their order. It ain't easy. Matthew "has" to sit next to Jesus but John is having none of it, because his birthday's Monday and Jesus promised. Simon's blowing into his hand and pretending he farted. Mark and James are pouting because I carded them. Thomas wants a Caesar salad but doesn't believe it when I tell him you can hardly taste the anchovies in the dressing. Paul says he's lactose intolerant and claims if there's sour cream in his borscht, it's coming out of my tip. Judas sits glowering because no one will split an appetizer with him, and the rest of them just giggle at my ASK ME ABOUT OUR KUGEL! button. The way they all behaved, I should have made them order off the children's menu.

If my ex-roommate hadn't just screwed me on last month's rent, believe me, I would've walked. I needed the shekels, but obviously none of these guys had ever waited tables. One of them actually snapped his fingers at me for a water refill. Not even to drink. He wanted to wash Jesus' feet! That's right, feet. Right at the table! It was enough to make Caligula nauseous. The only bev they ordered, one glass of house red. They all *split* it. Hello! Misers, party of thirteen.

At this point I think they saw I was getting pissed and realized I would be handling their food. If you think that kind of thing doesn't happen in good restaurants all the time, you're kidding yourself. We had a bartender, Isaac, who had a special drink recipe for rude customers. I'll give you a hint: The magic ingredient is yak piss. You think I'm lying? He's a Bedouin and believe me those people could give a shit.

After I got them settled down, everyone ordered the lamb, except John, who'd had lamb for lunch. You'd have thought we were feeding the lions the way they attacked that thing. I hope Jesus is planning some commandments on table manners. Anyway, we got through dinner but you can be sure I had Carlos prepare a fatty cut, even though they asked for lean.

As far as Jesus goes, we'd all heard about the miracles he performs, but he actually seemed pretty normal. I've had friends who get a little success and immediately turn into assholes, but he was cool about it. My friend's sister caught him when he did two nights in Thebes. She said it was okay. He bent some spoons and guessed that one guy in the audience was thinking about changing jobs, but she said he was better when he was still with the Lepers. Jesus definitely did no miracles at this dinner, although one of the waiters who got his autograph said it cleared up his sinuses.

No real pearls of wisdom either. Once, right before dessert, Jesus said to no one in particular, "Why do people park on a driveway and drive on a parkway?" It was *kind of* funny. Truthfully, Jesus spent most of the time asking people whether or not a beard would make him look smarter. There was a bit of a scuffle when Paul liked the idea but Judas thought it was trendy. I say cut the hair. Please. You're not a musician and it's very B.C.

Personally, when I found out one of those guys had betrayed Jesus, it didn't surprise me a bit. You can ask David son of Phil. I told him that night, "I would *not* trust these guys if I were Jesus." It's so obvious they're not really his friends. They're just hanging around him because he's famous. You should have seen them scatter when I brought the bill. "Can you cover me, Jesus?" "I'll get you next time, Jesus." "I gotta go drain the staff, Jesus!" I don't know how Jesus puts up with it. Poor guy probably had to walk on water just to get some peace and quiet.

Not that it kept me up nights. Let's face it. Messiahs come and go. Just last week I had a creep on table five who claimed that if I followed him, I would enjoy eternal joy in a place called Utah. He said I could have as many wives as I wanted but not caffeine. Get real. Me? Choose women over coffee? Please. Still, I *was* sorry to hear what happened to Jesus. He was a good tipper.

•   •   •

Editor's note: After this piece was published it was brought to our attention that Avram's manuscript is not the only document pertaining to the life and times of Jesus Christ. A work titled "The New Testament" was sent to our offices along with a large number of other pertinent volumes. We regret this oversight. Also, upon great scholarly review, Avram's manuscript was found to be written in Magic Marker, an implement not discovered until the early nineteen hundred and fifties. Again, our regrets.

DA VINCI: THE LOST NOTEBOOK

DA VINCI'S LOST NOTEBOOK, known from 1477 to 1485 as *da Vinci's Notebook,* was recently returned by Interpol agents who caught fraudulent art dealers, posing as fraudulent baseball card dealers, trying to pass the notebook off as a signed Sandy Koufax rookie card. Although da Vinci is dead and can no longer use the notebook, art historians hoped its return would settle their longstanding dispute over the notebook's disappearance. Some had argued that da Vinci had originally misplaced the notebook in 1485 after being startled by the Black Death, others were convinced the great artisan had left it in the back of a cab. Da Vinci himself was despondent over the loss until his death and was convinced Mona Lisa had something to do with it, often complaining to friends, "Look at her face. She knows something." Da Vinci never abandoned the search for the notebook and on his deathbed was heard to remark, "The hall closet! Son of a bitch!"

The Lost Notebook is a significant find because it details much of da Vinci's early work. It gives a glimpse into da Vinci's mind when he wasn't yet an acclaimed genius, just a creepy guy who sat alone in cafés writing in a notebook. The notebook contains some of da Vinci's early inventions, grocery lists and numerous "notes to self."

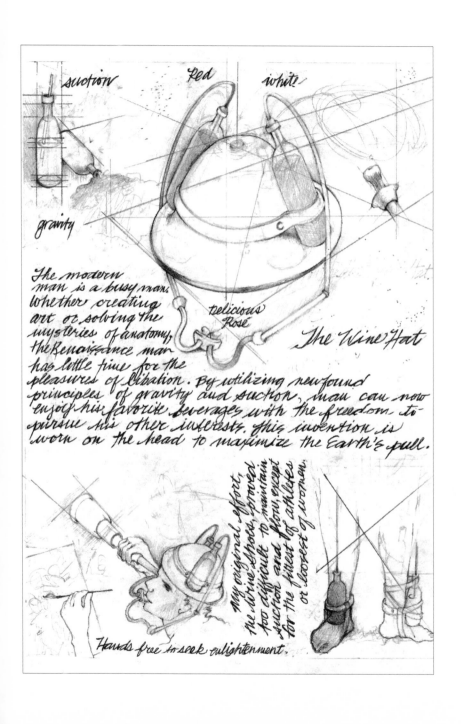

suction   Red   white!

gravity

delicious Rosé

The Wine Hat

The modern man is a busy man. Whether creating art or solving the mysteries of anatomy, the Renaissance man has little time for the pleasures of libation. By utilizing newfound principles of gravity and suction, man can now enjoy his favorite beverages with the freedom to pursue his other interests. This invention is worn on the head to maximize the Earth's pull.

My original effort, the Wine Shoe, proved too difficult to maintain suction and flow, except for the fittest of athletes or bravest of woman.

Hands free to seek enlightenment.

Some questions are insoluble. The evolution of man is such that all characteristics reflect a purpose to modern life. The reason of man. The thumb of man. All play a part in the origin of man to his present status. Why then has the primitive vestige of ass hair not vanished along with the tail and sloped forehead? Surely the advent of pantaloons would hasten its demise.

The hair on the body is proportional to the warmth necessary for comfort. Still the hair persists. Is a piece ill-designed for grooming. We must rectify!

The Ass Comb

Note to Self:
For unevenly distributed posterior hair, try the combover!

Tangled posterior hair reflects upon tangled reason.

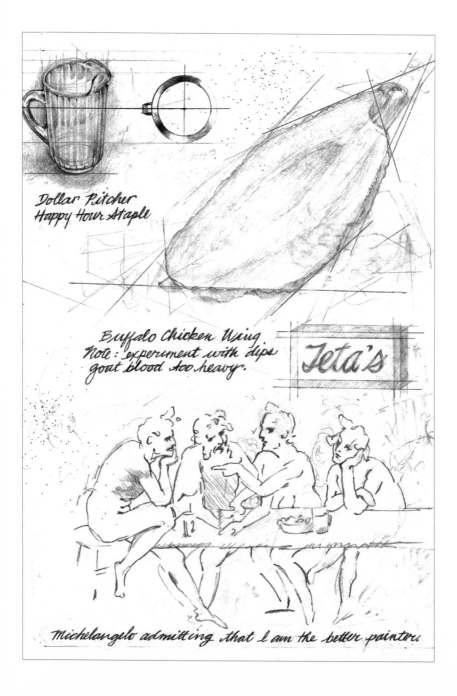

Dollar Pitcher
Happy Hour Staple

Buffalo Chicken Wing
Note: experiment with dips
goat blood too heavy.

Teta's

Michelangelo admitting that I am the better painter.

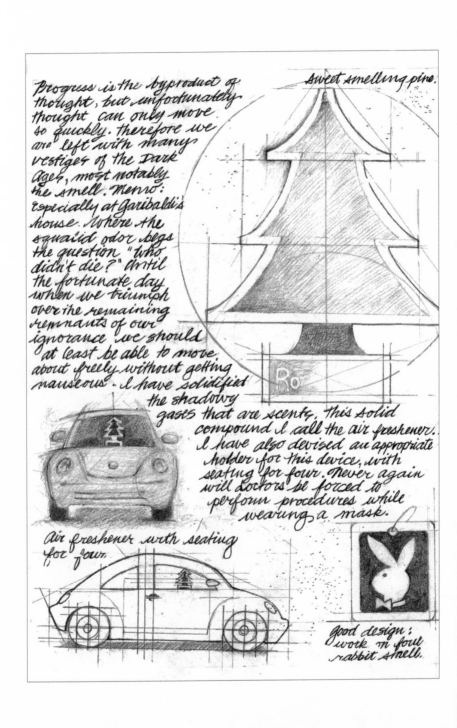

Progress is the byproduct of thought, but unfortunately thought can only move so quickly. therefore we are left with many vestiges of the Dark Ages, most notably the smell. Men: especially at Garibaldi's house. Where the squalid odor begs the question "who didn't die?" Until the fortunate day when we triumph over the remaining remnants of our ignorance we should at least be able to move about freely without getting nauseous. I have solidified the shadowy gases that are scents, this solid compound I call the air freshener. I have also devised an appropriate holder for this device, with seating for four. Never again will doctors be forced to perform procedures while wearing a mask.

Sweet smelling pine.

Air freshener with seating for four.

good design: work in foul rabbit smell.

The pursuit of sexual and edible pleasure is the greatest distraction for today's thinking man. If not for these seemingly insatiable drives, man would surely have furthered his cause of civilized understanding much faster, not to mention the financial strain of "pussy hunts". The scourges of Black Death, Typhoid, Bubonic Plague and Jews would surely be conquered if man's concentration could be swayed from food and ladies.

Then again, combining these two all consuming pursuits would seem like a sound business proposal for an eatery. Imagine one of Botticelli's full-breasted hotties, scantily clad, serving up a tasty helping of fried cheese or Calimari, all with your favorite brew. It's a can't miss proposition.

THE CULT

CONSIDERING THE MANY feats of leadership in the twentieth century, from Churchill's morale-rallying speeches in World War II to Martin Luther King Jr.'s marches for racial equality during the sixties, the ones that I find most impressive are the Jonestown Massacre and Heaven's Gate. While Churchill and King inspired loyalty and devotion, they had the benefit of real issues and problems to play on. Getting people to buckle down during World War II or walk a couple of blocks with you on a sunny day in Alabama are impressive indeed, but getting people to castrate or kill themselves for no reason other than you think you saw something about it in a dream is unparalleled control. Not to mention the fringe benefits the leader of a cult enjoys with his subject's wives.

I imagine myself as the persuasive leader of a messianic cult. Somewhat of a stretch considering I have yet to be able to sell off a box of Amway products I ordered in 1986. Still, would I have the strength? Would I be able to overcome my fear of death, zealous crowds and death by zealous crowds? Would I be able to keep a straight face as I took command of people's lives with rhetoric I thought of when I was high? Would I understand the intricacies of forming a tax-exempt organization? The uncertainty of the new millennium will create unprecedented opportunity in the field of messianic leaders. Will I be up to the challenge?

• • •

We begin in the back room of my cult's compound, a .05-acre structure known as my rent-controlled one-bedroom. My subjects have congregated on this day to witness our salvation. I have foretold a vision of the Rapture. At 4:00 P.M., Captain Crunch will spring to life from his resting place on the back of a cereal box and deliver us to our eternal bliss. It is 3:56 P.M. I sit with my two lieutenants and await the miracle or a gigantic ass kicking. The time is nigh, and I am fast running out of snacks.

LIEUTENANT JOHNSON: Leader...What a glorious day for our deliverance!

LIEUTENANT McSHANE: I was just thinking that. I wish I had said it before you had.

ME: (*distracted by the time*) Yes, yes. The day is glorious, although they say tomorrow's pollen count will be moderate to heavy.

LIEUTENANT JOHNSON: What care we of tomorrow, when salvation is but four minutes away.

ME: I'm just saying I would hate to go to our salvation with red itching eyes.

LIEUTENANT McSHANE: But the Captain will deliver us from our earthly afflictions. You said—

LIEUTENANT JOHNSON: He knows what he said. Why must you always nag? He knows we—

ME: Fellas, please. With the air conditioning out, the last thing I need is the two of you making a ruckus.

LIEUTENANT JOHNSON: Tell us again, for the last time, the story of Captain.

LIEUTENANT McSHANE: Yes, Leader, tell us.

ME: All right. But then you both have to finish unloading the dishwasher like I asked you yesterday.

LIEUTENANT JOHNSON: We're sorry, Leader. We just thought that with the Captain coming . . .

LIEUTENANT McSHANE: We would have no more use for earthly dishes.

ME: So you want the Captain to eat off dirty dishes. Our savior of saviors, and you can't take the time?

LIEUTENANTS JOHNSON AND McSHANE: We're sorry, Leader. Please forgive our sinful ways.

ME: All right, fine...get up. (*They begin to kiss my feet.*) C'mon. You're embarrassing me, you... (*they get up*) missed a spot. Anyhoo. The Captain was an all-powerful, benevolent leader. His people lived in a state of constant bliss, with a little sugar rush thrown in for good measure. One day, while his followers were being sinful and lazy and arguing with each other, a mean leprechaun accused the Captain of stealing his Lucky Charms. The leprechaun put a spell on the Captain, confining him until the righteous among us could pull the sword from the rock, showing the Captain we were worthy of receiving his good graces.

LIEUTENANT JOHNSON: Leader?

ME: Huh?

LIEUTENANT JOHNSON: I have a question. If the Captain is all-powerful...

ME: Uh huh.

LIEUTENANT JOHNSON: How could the leprechaun put a spell on him?

LIEUTENANT McSHANE: And what of the sword? I mean, I don't want to nitpick, but you never mentioned the sword before.

ME: You're gonna do this now? Huh? Three...two minutes to salvation and you're gonna do this now? Maybe you guys should have thought of this before you signed up, because if you're gonna nitpick I got a living room filled with believers that would love to be lieutenants. Remember, at Salvation, the lieutenants get to carry the Captain's hat.

LIEUTENANT McSHANE: No, Leader. Please don't be angry. It's just ... I had never heard that thing about the sword before.

ME: Well, I just remembered it. Besides, you had no trouble swallowing the cereal box come to life part.

LIEUTENANT McSHANE: That's true.

LIEUTENANT JOHNSON: And when the Captain comes he will relieve our earthly afflictions?

ME: Bingo.

LIEUTENANT JOHNSON: This cursed cleft chin will finally be gone.

ME: I keep telling you. That's considered a positive feature.

LIEUTENANT McSHANE: And what of my leprosy?

ME: Your what?

LIEUTENANT McSHANE: Leprosy.

ME: I thought that was dermatitis.

LIEUTENANT McSHANE: (*Showing his arms*) This is dermatitis. (*Lifting up his shirt*) This is leprosy.

ME: Oh my God (*furiously washing any exposed skin*). I hugged you in the Circle of Knowledge yesterday!

LIEUTENANT McSHANE: Fear not for me, Leader, for the Captain—

ME: Yeah, yeah. I get it. And I can do without the comforting touch on the shoulder, okay? And if you'd please just get off the chair, nothing personal. I just had them redone and it cost a fortune ... and I'll take the drinking glass, please ... thank you.

(*From the other room a group chant begins.*)

OTHER ROOM: CAPTAIN, WE ARE READY. 10 ... 9 ... 8 ...

ME: My watch still says 3:58. Fucking imitation Rolex. (*I bang the watch on the table and then put it up to my ear.*)

LIEUTENANT JOHNSON: Come, Leader, let us join the others so the Captain will see our solidarity.

ME: You guys go. I still have that ... thing ... in the oven. Wouldn't want the Captain's chicken to get dry.

LIEUTENANTS JOHNSON AND McSHANE: All right. See you in Nirvana.

ME: Right.

(*They exit. The chant goes on. 3 ... 2 ... 1. Then all is silent. Except for the sound of me trying to pry open a window. The silence endures ... and then ... the Lieutenants re-enter the room.*)

LIEUTENANT JOHNSON: Uhh, Leader ... can we have a word with you, please?

ME: (*coming back in from the window*) Huh. Oh! In a sec. I thought I felt a draft. See this cracked rubber around the windowpane?...Hey, how's the Captain?

LIEUTENANT McSHANE: Everyone would like a word with you in the front... *now.*

ME: Sure, sure. (*They grab me and drag me into the front room.*) Hey, everybody! What can I do you for?

FOLLOWER #1: It is 4:02. And still the Captain remains on the box. Smirking at us.

ME: 4:02. Right. Right...Oh my God. It's Daylight Saving Time, isn't it? In the Land of Plenty it's still 3:02. Silly mistake. I can't believe I—

FOLLOWER #1: You lied to us, Leader. You took advantage of us.

ME: Now let's not start hurling accusations. I mean, who among us can really cast the first stone? Lying, taking advantage. Those are serious allega—

FOLLOWER #1: You slept with my wife.

FOLLOWER #2: You slept with my wife and daughter. (*A clamor arises from the followers.*)

ME: All right now, settle down, people. Remember, I'm still the one making up the seating chart for the rocket ship (*They quiet.*) Good. Now, I'll admit, James—

FOLLOWER #2: Paul.

ME: Right, Paul. Paul, I'll admit you definitely took one for the team on that one. Heh, heh. Well. Are we out of onion dip? Let me run out and grab some quick, because the Captain's going to be here in about (*checking watch*) fifty-five minutes and you know he'll be hungry and . . . (*They stop me from going, and gather around me ominously.*) Hey, c'mon. Why the long faces? The Captain's a little late. Christ. The guy's been on a box for—

FOLLOWER #3: You took all I had in the world. You destroyed my family. All I did was ask you for directions and before I knew what hit me, you had ruined me with your lies of a promised land of Crunchberries and honey . . . and you slept with me.

ME: Whoa there, Phil. (*Everyone begins to push in.*) I categorically deny I slept with this guy.

FOLLOWER #3: Thursday night . . . by the washing machine.

ME: Oh my God . . . You've got soft hands.

FOLLOWER #4: Get him!!

(*General mayhem ensues. Lamps break, blood is shed, feelings are hurt.*)

ME: People, please! Settle down! This is a sublet. Now listen. I know you're disappointed that the Captain didn't show us the way to eternal salvation, but we still have cable till the end of the month, so let's show a little restraint here.

LIEUTENANT JOHNSON: Perhaps the Captain knew there were skeptics among us. Perhaps this is why he has forsaken us.

ME: Boom! Exactly. Couldn't have put it better myself. Damn skeptics. Maybe if you people hadn't balked at the bathroom tax none of this would—

LIEUTENANT McSHANE: A suicide pact will convince the Captain of our sincerity. A suicide pact led by our leader. To the medicine cabinet! The Leader will die and we shall follow.

(*The crowd is aroused and moves toward the bathroom.*)

ME: Whoa. Whoa. Slow down there, chief. I mean, suicide . . . we could get in a lot of trouble for that. Besides, there's barely enough Valium in there to keep me calm when I fly. Hell, when I even think about flying . . .

(*The crowd moves to force the drugs into my system.*)

LIEUTENANT JOHNSON: Suicide is the only way!

ME: You never heard of a letter-writing campaign?

FOLLOWER #3: I will join you!

(*All join in.*)

FOLLOWER #4: I will join you!

FOLLOWER #5: I found a nickel!

(*As the pills are placed on my lips, I break free.*)

ME: Stop. This is madness! (*The crowd hushes at my fervor.*) I can't take these without juice.

FOLLOWER #1: You're stalling.

ME: Not true. If they were caplets I might be able to squeeze them down, but ...

FOLLOWER #2: You're a staller and a liar.

ME: Look. You're all really mad at me, but ... You wanted this. You needed this. It was your weakness that made this all possible. You didn't want to take responsibility for your own lives. You had to look to a savior to make it all better for you. I didn't do this to you, you did it to yourselves. I asked for your money and your wives ... and that guy's daughter ... and—

FOLLOWER #3: And me.

ME: And Phil here, although I could have sworn ... anyway. You gave to me willingly. You wanted to believe in an easy solution to the complex stresses and anxieties of your lives. I saved you from yourselves.

(*All is quiet in the room ... finally:*)

FOLLOWER #2: Let's kick his ass!!

(*A warlike shriek goes up and the mob attacks.*)

ME: Wait! Stop! Ow! Don't pull, it's not a toupee! ... Oh my God! It's THE CAPTAIN!

(*The room goes silent as all eyes shift to the cereal box.*)

ME: See? Do you see! The Captain hasn't moved, but for that one brief moment, we all believed again. We all believed in the possibility of our salvation. (*Heads nodding, the believers are contemplating.*) Remember those days. The believing days. Those were good times, huh—uhhhh... (*A steel-toed boot is applied to my midsection. As my former disciples descend upon me like hungry hyenas, tearing me limb from limb, I think of only two things: I'm going to lose my security deposit and sugared cereals are a death sentence.*)

FIVE UNDER FIVE

WHO AMONG US will build that bridge to the twenty-first century? Who among us will fail to identify the correct cultural trends and end up living under that bridge— uninformed trolls who were told repeatedly that Mehndi designs were in, yet whose feet and hands are still horribly unadorned? Magazines have been most generous in identifying the "30 people under 30" who will lead us stylishly, entertainingly and politically into this grand new millennium. We've been handed a blueprint. Those with a keen eye will never again find themselves bringing a white trash seventies theme party to a crashing halt with the question "Tibet's not free?" Magazine editors have paved the rough road into the year 2000.

Then what? Recent "People to Watch" articles only take us at best through the year 2005. Are we then to stand alone, looking out into the abyss of our future ... unguided by the cutting edge of the trendsetters? Who will be the most powerful television executive? The next generation's favorite author? What will our models be wearing? Who will be our models' favorite author? The boomers will die. Generation X will develop prostate trouble. Generation Y will probably still be fine, but as they approach middle age, will we be as interested in what they're doing? Who will be there to inform us in the years 2015–2025?

Help is on the way. A research team from Condé Nast has identified five people to watch under the age of five. They feel these extraordinary people will be at the forefront of our early-to-mid-twenty-first-century cultural trends. The Fab Five is a diverse group, cutting across a variety of demographic categories. Yet they all share one exceptional truth: All of the "Five to Watch" selections should be around twenty to thirty years of age during the years 2015–2025. So whether it be politics, media, science or the humanities, the researchers concluded that at least one of their selections should be involved in one of those pursuits in some capacity or another. So it is my pleasure, in conjunction with the fine people at Condé Nast, to introduce The Five to Watch Under Five.

CHELSEA JAMESON

AGE: 5

BIRTHPLACE: Atlanta, Georgia

EDUCATION: Captain Jack's Toddlerama, certified tumbler, Gymboree.

POWER SPOT: The sandbox at Captain Jack's. "Everyone goes there after lunch. It's fun to play."

LESSONS LEARNED: "If someone asks you to get into their van you shouldn't because they are probably bad."

INSPIRATION: "What do you mean?"

Our experts felt that women would play an important role in the early to mid twenty-first century. While Chelsea is not yet a woman, it appears certain that within fifteen to twenty years, she will be. Only five, Chelsea already has a boyfriend, Jake, and her mother believes she is very socially oriented—unlike her brother Max, three, who is very shy and will likely never appear on any list, except one detailing various shy people. Her parents feel, and we agree, that Chelsea could be at the forefront of some field of communications, perhaps TV, either on camera or off, most likely on. Or a ballerina.

MICHAEL GREEN

AGE: 4 ½

BIRTHPLACE: Manhattan

EDUCATION: Home schooled.

POWER SPOT: Temple Beth El, 68th and West End. "It gets very crowded and hot. I like jelly but I'm allergic."

LESSONS LEARNED: "I might never amount to anything. Especially if I keep it up, mister."

FAVORITE FOOD: Anything binding.

Although only four and a half, Michael suffers from anxiety disorders befitting a much more successful older man. From irritable bowel syndrome to pattern baldness to an allergic reaction caused by the underside of his own skin, Michael has all the physical manifestations of the high achiever. He hasn't achieved as of yet, but our expert panel attributes much of that to Michael's more than three-year confinement in an oxygen steam tent. You need look no further than his name to find his potential. Michael changed it from his given name of Hyman Yid because "I didn't want people to get the wrong idea . . . My head itches." Michael's a comer, and even his parents' assertion that "he'll catch his death of cold" doesn't dissuade us from putting him on the list. If he survives to 2020, he's a high-powered executive waiting to happen . . . or a serial killer.

MAGGIE LYNN PRATT

AGE: 8

BIRTHPLACE: Hollywood, California

EDUCATION: Anson "Potsie" Williams Institute of Playacting, Paul Spielberg's Dreamworkshop, Emotions for Kids.

POWER SPOT: The children's menu at Orso. "I love Macauley's Mac and Cheese and the Curly Sue Curly Fries."

INSPIRATION: "My family and the rush of artistic impression—um . . . expression? . . . is that good, Daddy?"

Although Maggie is not technically under five we included her on this list because her father, a powerful publicist, felt we should. Maggie's "classic look and effortless charm" make her "a sure bet for stardom." We did not meet Maggie but saw from her headshot that she might be very pretty when she gets older. If not, she will be made pretty by state-of-the-art surgical procedures, depending upon the societal norms for attractiveness at the time. Maggie's actual abilities at this point are unclear, but rest assured, by the year 2015 she will be very famous and powerful. Maggie Lynn Pratt was unavailable for comment at the printing of this article.

CARY STREISAND RENT

AGE: 45 months
BIRTHPLACE: Cryotech Institute's underground bunker, somewhere near the Rocky Mountains.
EDUCATION: A 10GB RAM upgradable hard drive with 466MHz processor implanted in his brain.
POWER SPOT: Underneath a high-powered microscope. "Stop poking me with needles ... stop it."
INSPIRATIONAL SAYING: "I am not an animal."

Cary was created 45 months ago by the Cryotech Institute. Funded by a rich gay couple from the Silicon Valley, Cary represents a new wave of generational trendsetters not born purely of human reproduction. Cary's the product of a genetic marriage between a high-powered MIT physics genius, a top Broadway lyricist and, quite accidentally, a rare breed of long-haired Persian cat. Watching Cary play with his sterilized toys you can easily see he has the carefree rambunctiousness of any young boy with an enormously oversized cranium, eight nipples and a tail. At just three years and some Cary is already an accomplished physicist and neurologist with incredible taste in window treatments. If the government prevails in their lawsuit, he will also soon be working on futuristic weapons systems. I think you'll agree the only thing that can stop our fourth member of this honored list is his own imagination . . . and the distracting lure of a ball of yarn . . . or if he tries to sleep lying down like a normal boy.

There was no consensus on the final member of the Five Under Five list, but the research team agreed it would be someone Asian or black. Next month: The Fifty Most Beautiful People You Will Never Have Sex With.

THE RECIPE

THE FOLLOWING RECIPE comfortably serves three to four thousand with room for a television viewing audience. For smaller events cut the production number and halve the presenters.

START WITH:

ONE VIBRANT, ELABORATELY COSTUMED DANCE NUMBER SET TO A MEDLEY OF POPULAR HITS. AS MUSIC SWELLS TO A CRESCENDO BRING THE DANCING TO AN ABRUPT CLIMAX. END MUSIC. ADD AUDIENCE APPLAUSE AND BOOMING INTRODUCTION OF THE WELL-RESPECTED, ACERBIC HOST. PLAY HOST'S SIGNATURE THEME SONG. CONTINUE APPLAUSE. CROSS HOST TO PODIUM. END MUSIC AND APPLAUSE.

HOST:

General greetings and a query as to the audience's well-being. Affirmation of audience's well-being. Statement of own well-being. Survey of surroundings. Improvised analogy comparing surroundings to different surroundings. Sarcastic jab at expected length of proceedings.

PAUSE FOR LAUGHTER.

HOST:

Confusion about actions of government officials. Statement of proposed personal action if given opportunity to govern.

PAUSE FOR LAUGHTER. IF LAUGHTER IS NOT FORTHCOMING

HOST:

Recognition of power and ability among audience. Statement of fear over possible consequences failure to entertain said powers would entail.

IF LAUGHTER IS FORTHCOMING

HOST:

Query as to audience's familiarity with behavior of recently disgraced cultural icon. Incredulity and displeasure at said behavior. Command for icon to discontinue behavior. Statement of new product created as a result of icon's behavior.

PAUSE FOR LAUGHTER.

HOST:

Praise of audience for responsiveness and sense of humor. Query as to their readiness for program's continuation. Introduction of two participants who will begin process of bestowing honors: an unattractive, humorous male renowned for his portrayal of other unattractive, humorous males, and a female of great physical beauty who has achieved fame for her skill in walking while wearing newly designed expensive clothing.

ADD MUSIC AND APPLAUSE AS HOST LEAVES STAGE. BRING HUMOROUS MAN AND BEAUTIFUL WOMAN TO PODIUM. STOP APPLAUSE AND MUSIC.

MAN:

(*To woman*) Compliment concerning sexual attractiveness.

WOMAN:

(*Stilted, as though reading aloud*) Acceptance and return of compliment.

MAN:

Lurid sexual innuendo. Winking proposition with broad physical gesturing.

WOMAN:

(*Stilted, as though reading aloud*) Unusually intelligent rebuke of said proposition.

MAN:

Surprise at intelligence of rebuke. Feigned lack of disappointment at rebuke. Conceited statement of missed sexual opportunity for the woman, again with broad physical gesturing.

PAUSE FOR LAUGHTER AMONG AUDIENCE AND PRESENTERS.

WOMAN:

Query as to the identity of the author of previously read statements and indictment of their ability. List of possible honorees.

STAND MAN AND WOMAN ASIDE. SHOW EACH POSSIBLE HONOREE PERFORMING THE TASK FOR WHICH THEY ARE TO BE HONORED. SHOW ALL PRESENT POSSIBLE HONOREES IN THE AUDIENCE WAITING FOR THE RESULT OF THEIR EFFORT.

MAN:

(*Opening a sealed correspondence*) Announcement of the one true honoree.

GREAT REJOICING AMONG THE BELIEVERS IN THE VERDICT. REFLECTION AND BITTER QUESTIONING AMONG THE OTHERS. BRING THE HONORED ONE TO THE STAGE TO BE LAUDED. A FEMALE OF SURGICALLY ENHANCED SEXUAL ATTRACTIVENESS

HANDS A TOTEM OF ACHIEVEMENT TO THE HONOREE, WHO GRASPS IT WITH GREAT REVERENCE. AUDIENCE APPLAUSE.

HONOREE:

Breathless surprise. Self-effacing remark concerning previous outcomes of similar events. Feigned lack of preparation. Expression of gratitude for inventors of the totem as well as constituents of totem. Expression of gratitude for believers in verdict. Expression of gratitude for members of blood lineage and Supreme Exalted Being. Expression of gratitude for creators of shown task. Expression of regret concerning those who have not received expressions of gratitude. Statement of nonharmful intent for those who have not received gratitude. Plea for group subjected to persecution to no longer be subject to said persecution.

SWELL MUSIC.

HONOREE:

Regret at musical interruption and self-criticism at lack of organizational and communication skills. Sudden remembrance of those still in need of expressions of gratitude.

DIM MUSIC SLIGHTLY.

HONOREE:

Fear of further recrimination if closing remarks are

not forthcoming. Hurried expression of love for those present, viewing or being.

SWELL MUSIC. AUDIENCE APPLAUSE. HONOREE IS ESCORTED AWAY BY PRESENTERS WHILE DISPLAYING TOTEM TO THE AUDIENCE. HOST APPEARS.

HOST:

Perceptive remark concerning unexpected length and emotional tenor of honoree's presentation. Example of previous presentation famous for such characteristics.

PAUSE FOR LAUGHTER.

HOST:

Introduction of corpulent woman, well known for recognizing and satirizing her physical condition, and an adolescent known for contracting a fatal illness.

REPEAT AS NECESSARY.

Editor's note: This ancient recipe was found in 1982 by archeologists on a Peruvian dig, outside the fabled Mayan city of Atachupulay... ay. It is but one of the many startling discoveries included in a new work by Erich Van Daniken entitled Weird, Huh? *continuing his exhaustive efforts to prove the existence of alien visitations. This recipe, translated from its original Mayan glyph in 1985 by a really smart lady, was printed on parchment that dates back four thousand years. The parchment is made from the intestines of rare Andes mountain* goats and although it was not dated scientifically, the feeling within the scientific community was, you had to be very primitive to still be writing on the guts and shit inside of a goat. Originally thought to be a recipe for using the rest of the goat, it soon turned out to be a more important find. The recipe details all the necessary ingredients of a successful entertainment industry awards show—a full three to four thousand years before the existence of entertainment! Could the Mayans, a tribe that had only barely mastered the use of a sundial, have predicted this phenomenon . . . or did visitors arrive from the heavens bearing the knowledge of an advanced civilization? Perhaps the truth will never be known.

THE DEVIL AND WILLIAM GATES

IT'S A STORY they tell in the Pacific Northwest, where Washington State meets up with what is left of the Wilderness Provinces formerly known as Canada.

Yes, William Gates is dead and buried—or at least he died. Folks say they converted his remains into binary code and shot him out over the World Wide Web. Some say it was the work of his most committed disciples, others that his remains just reverted back to their natural state of being. Whichever school of thought you go by, most folks agree that he still haunts almost every transaction of business takin' place. They say when you go to the ATM and it tells you you ain't got sufficient funds, or if you swipe your personal ID cyberpass, the one built into your eyeball, into your own front door and it still denies you access, you can stop and take a listen . . . and you'll hear ol' Billy gigglin' and wipin' his runny nose on the sleeve of his all-weather reversible Lands' End parka. And they say you can visit his Web site at BillGates.com and type in "Bill Gates . . . Billy Gates!" and sure enough the keyboard'll start to shiverin' and the screen will jump to life and a kind of annoyed, not very deep voice will answer—if you have the model with the voice actualizer—"Hey, neighbor, how stands the Microsoft Union?" And you better answer that "She stands as she stood, innovative, dominant and up one and an eighth per share" or a smallish, soft-skinned hand is liable to shoot out of the screen and delete you. At least that's how they told it to me as a boy.

You see, for a while, Bill Gates was the biggest man in the country . . . heck, the world. There wasn't one millisecond of a man's day that Bill Gates didn't have some or total control over. From your morning commute to the hot milk and biscuit you'd put down before bed, it was all run through the auspices of Bill's say-so. It's been said that with the simple touch of a key he could give you explosive diarrhea or an orgasm that made you feel like the Lord Almighty was fellating you. They said Bill wasn't much to look at. Bookish, with wire-rim glasses and the kind of haircut that brings peals of laughter from old mates as they're scanning through your downloaded eighth-grade yeardiskette. They said he wasn't much to listen to either. But he sure could ruin people. They said the entire state of Florida was deleted because Bill felt it wasn't tidy, sticking out the way it did into the Atlantic Ocean.

But this tale begins before all that. Before Bill Gates was ever President or World CEO. Before Manhattan was converted into a maximum security prison. Before man had lost control of society to Apes, getting it back, only to lose it again to Elk, then Otters, then getting it back again. This story begins, if you'll dare believe, at a time when Bill Gates was just another name in what they used to call the Phone Book.

In the month of May, in the year of nineteen hundred and seventy-five, in the time when the Earth still revolved around the sun, Bill Gates was floundering in a town called Seattle. He wasn't a bad man, but an unlucky one. If neighbors had their hours cut at work, he got fired. If neighbors got a sore throat, he got mono; if neighbors did coke and fornicated all night to the strains of KC and the Sunshine Band, Bill got his ass whupped by the big retarded kid who lived next door. Being a creative sort, he even tried his hand at inventin' something that might be his ticket to success. It was a product called "317 Flushes Blue," a tonic to keep the ceramic area where people used to urinate fresh smellin'. But wouldn't you know that around the same time another fella came up with the same product. Exceptin' this fella's lasted 2,000 flushes! Ol' Bill saw red when he found out about that one.

Here he was nearly twenty years old, little to no body hair, still livin' in his parents' care and not a speck of relief in sight. In disgust he threw down his totebag and cursed to the heavens: "I swear . . . it's enough to make a man sell his soul to the Devil! And I would too!!" As he uttered the blasphemy a horrendous crash arose from the Earth and Bill jumped back, expecting the Devil himself would appear. He didn't. The noise came from the tote bag, wherein lay his unsolved Rubik's Cube, now smashed in anger. He was relieved. But still, roller-skating home, he felt a bit queer about what he had uttered.

As it got toward evening, when it seemed no notice had been taken, Bill felt his fear ease, even permitting himself a quick game of Dungeons & Dragons with some local pre-teens. But as you know, a cry to the Dark One rarely goes unnoticed. Sure enough, next morning, a quiet, oddly hand-some fella drove up in one of them old-style, gas-fueled Japanese model automobiles, asking for one William Gates the Third.

Bill's folks didn't care for the looks of the stranger, being that he had hooves, horns, smelled like burnt cake and disemboweled their dog when it growled at him. Bill knew this was Beelzebub himself, but told his folks the stranger was an old school chum who'd been kicked out of the Merchant Marines on account of his being gay. That eased their curiosity and Bill and the stranger went up to Bill's room to settle the business at hand.

Bill entered the bedroom with trepidation. He knew the Devil lorded it over an empire of unspeakable evil, and had also caused Flip Wilson's Geraldine to do some incredibly sassy things. But today the Devil was all business. The fiend pulled out a rectangular object, no bigger than a common notebook, flipped it open and tapped a pointed finger onto its lettered keyboard. The doohickey hummed to life and Ol' Bill about jumped through a window in fright. "Spare my life, Satan. I'll serve you however you please!" implored Bill, cowering from the eerie luminescence of the machine's face. "Fear not" was the Beast's calm reply, "For you have many years of prosperity ahead, before your bill comes due." But Bill still trembled in the presence of this powerful, yet portable instrument. "And as for this," the Devil continued, "it's merely a convenience. You have no idea of the paperwork generated by the selling of even one soul." With that he tapped again and a second machine began spewing a fully formed contract of servitude. The terms called for a prosperous period equal to Bill's life of misfortune to date plus five, twenty-five years in total. It was decided Bill's fortune was to come at the hands of the very object that had caused his great fright, in part because the Devil saw Bill's fascination with the product and also because the Devil was a fan of irony, O. Henry being the first author he ever signed. The deal was consummated with saliva rather than blood, a final generosity extended on account of Bill's squeamish nature, it being common knowledge he became nauseous even cutting his toenails.

After that, life was no longer a chore for Bill Gates. Armed with a computer operating system and the magic that only true evil can bring, his days became one triumph after another. Intoxicated by this prosperous turn, Bill soon forgot the horrific mortgage which would be the cost. Days became weeks, weeks became years and years . . . generally stayed years. Bill Gates became rich, took a wife and bought, among other things, a large-screen TV. He was happy. Happier than a virtual hedgehog in a computerized game of skill, he would say in moments of mirth. He was much admired, even by the Beast, who had rarely seen a client so industriously fulfill his prophecy. But as the twenty-five years drew to a close, the shadow of his ill-fated bargain grew larger, and Bill Gates began to dread the day of the Stranger's return. His only comfort was the hope that his overwhelming success would buy some time, a hedge against his demise. Wouldn't he be a more effective tool for the Devil in his present state of power? Bill Gates vowed that when his time arrived, he would be ready with a powerful leveraged buyout package the Devil himself wouldn't be able to reject.

And his time did arrive. Sooner rather than later, for no time moves as quickly as that of the condemned. On a rainy afternoon twenty-five years to the day after that fateful meeting, a mysterious stranger once again appeared on Bill Gates's doorstep. He arrived in a style befitting the reclamation of what had become his most successful contract. A sleek black Mercedes, tuxedo and luxurious black cape, the only oddity being the rainbow-colored umbrella hat Satan favored during inclement weather. Bill Gates was ready.

No sooner had the Stranger sated himself at the wondrous banquet Bill had prepared for him, enjoyed the flown-in vocal gymnastics of Luciano Pavarotti and viewed some classic *Star Trek* episodes from Bill's vast laser-disc collection, than Bill launched into his defense. Prepared with the latest Microsoft graphics interface, the defense included pie charts, projections and statistics, all prepared to persuade evil incarnate of Bill's continued worth. But I imagine it will come as no surprise to the reader that among other faults, Patience is not Satan's strong suit. As Bill launched into the climax of his presentation—unlimited stock options—the Devil leaped from his chair with an angry wave of his cape. "Enough!" cried the Beastmaster. "A deal is a deal!"

But the Devil need not have uttered a word of convincing, for Bill Gates now saw, in all its horror, the folly of his attempt. For as the Devil rose, a small moth fluttered weakly from under his cape. It cried out in a pitiful nasal voice, "Help me, Neighbor Gates! For the love of God help me. This man has incarcerated me without due process. Without a Prima Facie Writ of . . ." And with that the voice went silent, snatched by the Devil and placed back into confinement. "My God . . . that . . . that was Alan Dershowitz's voice I heard," said a shocked Bill Gates. "I'm sure of it."

"So it was" was the smug reply.

"But I just saw him on *Geraldo*. . . . You . . . you have his soul?" trembled Bill, doubly frightened, for the legal maneuvering and general pestering of Dershowitz was his Plan B for breaking the contract.

The Devil nodded. Gates listened again and heard the unmistakable voice of Kathie Lee Gifford singing classic Gilbert and Sullivan from beneath the Beast's robe. "And Kathie Lee?" Bill wept aloud, "her too?!" The Beast laughed, "No, no. That's just part of the torture." Gates shuddered. The bleak future suddenly overcame him. He begged and was granted one more day to put his affairs in order. The Devil left, assured of his triumph, and Bill Gates stood alone in his mansion . . . looking paler than usual.

Now, fine reader, you may justifiably assume our tale ends here. Another example of avarice and deceit leading man astray, and ultimately destroying him. But to jump to that conclusion would underestimate the considerable wiles of one Bill Gates. Surely the day looked bleak, but Bill Gates had taken notice of details. Details that, with a bit of ingenuity, might just free him from eternal damnation. A lesser man might have surrendered to the inevitable, but as history teaches us, Chairman Gates was no ordinary man. He stepped into his virtual office and got to work.

The Devil awoke the next morning to what he assumed would be a day of crowning achievement. But oddities haunted his every move. He had checked into a downtown Seattle Hyatt Regency the previous night. There had been lodging more conveniently situated to the Gates estate but Satan had stayed in Hyatts before and trusted the quality of their spacious rooms and competent if not spectacular service. He would often refer to their Sunday Chef's Choice Brunch as a "wicked indulgence." When the Beast of Beasts went to check out of his suite, however, he was quite disturbed at what he found. Being a Regency Club member, he normally breezed through the checkout process, but a nagging suspicion told him to be more thorough on this occasion. Sure enough, his computerized bill contained an unfounded movie charge. The bill claimed the Devil had indulged in the Guest's Choice Pay-Per-View film *Jingle All the Way*, ironically starring two of his clients. After clearing up the discrepancy, he asked that the balance of his bill be left on his credit card. Those familiar with the domain of Bill Gates know what happened next. The hotel informed Satan his credit card had been reported as stolen. They refused the card and issued the further warning that unless payment was immediately forthcoming, they would have no recourse but to call the authorities. Lucifer was livid. He had the cash, but that wasn't the point. Every time he used that credit card he also received Frequent Flyer miles from American, which he relied on for travel upgrades. And besides, the card was his and he hadn't reported it missing. Satan, not having the time to argue his point, paid cash and stormed off, swearing vengeance, as well as taking a silent vow to, in the future, take his business elsewhere.

Now you or I might have taken stock at this point, questioning the origin of such odd shenanigans, but not the Beast. So enraged by the event was he, and so focused on his next task, no thought of betrayal occurred to him. That is, until he saw the flashing police lights in his rearview mirror. And no amount of pleading, bargaining or self-righteous indignation could dissuade the officers from their charge of grand theft auto. Even down at the station, Satan hoped his fingerprints would clarify the issue. He felt sure that once they saw his true identity, their initial shock would give way to repentance and panicked cries for forgiveness and mercy. But wouldn't you know it. When the police ran the Beast's prints through the computer, the readout showed the perpetrator to be not the Lord of Darkness, but a crack-addicted prostitute from San Diego named Ruth Marx. The police said no charges were going to be pressed, thanks in whole to the generosity of the car's owner ... Mr. Bill Gates. They let Satan walk, with the admonition to "keep her nose clean," but that wouldn't be a worry. The fight had gone out of the old demon.

You may be wondering why the Master of All Things Evil didn't perpetrate his sinister craft during any of these harassments. Burn the hotel to cinders and turn the cop into a baby's anus. Excellent query, but you forget a crucial point. Lucifer, like his archrival, God, relies on belief for his power. To deny his identity or existence is to render him powerless. It's the one loophole to his omnipotence and Ol' Bill took full advantage. The Devil—or, as the police said, Ruth—knew he had been bested, and now he had no choice but to go to his conqueror, hat in hand.

Well, friends, the legend has it that around midnight, May 11, in the year two thousand A.D., exactly twenty-five years and a day after their first meeting, Satan arrived at the estate of one William Gates the Third, Chairman of Microsoft Industries. Worn out by his troubles, not to mention the long walk, the demon formerly known as Satan wordlessly handed over his horns, and a new, even more powerful, entity was unleashed onto the world. As for Ol' Bill, well, any schoolkid can recite from rote his record of World Domination from that point forward, but the Devil? That's a little less clear. One version had him wandering off through the wilderness, never stopping, never sleeping for fear of prosecution on drug charges. But the truth, the truth is even more chilling. Bill Gates was so merciless in victory, he sentenced the poor Devil to be a proctor in an MTV chat room on America Online. The Devil, under the screen name Ol' Scratch, spent his remaining years monitoring conversations that sought to determine who actually ruled: Ozzy or Kurt Cobain. He died miserable and insane.

And that's the story as told to me when I was a boy. If you've got more time, kind reader, perhaps you'd like to hear the tale of "The Hooters Girl and Theodore Turner"?

VINCENT AND THEO ON AOL

IT HAS BEEN said that online computer services will bring back literacy and the ancient art of letter writing. I ventured into some America Online chat rooms to test the hypothesis with one of history's finest practitioners of this lost form of communication, Vincent van Gogh. I signed on to AOL as VincentVG and began typing. Please excuse the spelling and syntax errors contained in this piece. These are the actual transcripts of my chat room experiences. Cybernames have been changed to protect the innocent.

MAY 11

AOL PEOPLE CHAT, 12:25 P.M.

VINCENTVG: Dearest Theo. Oh the human form! How splendid to draw a living breathing creature. How treacherous as well. Still, to capture the movement and emotion, the colors of our lives...

JENNY34C: How big a man are you?

TRIPPY2000: WA SUP WITCHA

RRRUFFF: Are you blonde lassie

JENNY34C: Height I mean.

VINCENTVG: As I live and breathe Theo, it becomes more apparent that no matter what the cost, I must capture all that I feel.

POLLYWANT: I am new to this and am enjoying.

ELVIS666: I live in California.

LEVER180: 5-11

ASHFOR145: im a youngin

JENNY34C: I forgot, I'm 5–7

ADAM12: SEND ME A PIC

ADAM12: SEND ME A PIC

ADAM12: SEND ME A PIC

VincentVG: Once again, only the blackness that is me can halt the work I am called upon to do. Today was a good day. I am still not able to eat, but stood twice and hope soon to wave to the young nurse who comes frequently to give Messerlich his enemas.

TheTodster: Is anyoune her e naughty?

Lever180: u look great ffrom here.

Adam12: OK. IF NO ONE SENDS ME A PIC SOON I SWEAR

VincentVG: It no longer matters if I live or die, for now I am sure my life is as it should be. But still, paints are expensive and I believe I am being charged for this service by the hour so anything you can spare dear Theo. I know how tiresome I have become. Yesterday I declined an invitation to see myself naked.

LIOCO: Any fun guys in here?

MAY 14

MTV CHAT ROOM, 9:17 P.M.

VincentVG: Theo. Fear overwhelms me. This confounded machine has stolen my remaining resolve. I spent the morning conversing amongst "The Breakfast Club," midmorning in "Brunch Buddies," the afternoon in "The Best Li'l Chathouse" and evening in "The Saloon." Before I'm swept into the "Powertools Lounge" I plead for your help!

HEAVYMTL: Who likes sublime press 22

BRADGMAN: if you like will smith's getting jiggy wit it press 11

RADGRRRRL: MYA IS COOL AND PRAS

CLOVE: 22

VINCENTVG: I believe Gauguin was right about me. I am a failure. Three days ago I mistakenly ordered thousands of Bonsai trees while trying to download Netscape.

SLAYER15: ANY GIRL WANNA CHAT WITH A 15/M

HEAVYMTL: 22

INTROBERT: 11

JACKMEOFF: WASSUP SPEED DDDDD

BO44FF: 11

MMMMM7: AMEN 2 THAT

LBMICH22A: 22

VINCENTVG: I believe the Impressionists are finished. Monet has betrayed us. He has moved to Pointillism and then to connecting the points. He tells me it's a horse but I am too stupid to see it.

RевEL565: Slayer15 im me if you're a fine punker or skater

GIRLIEEEE: "its all about me"

POOKıE33: any1 inTA Fiona Apple

B1OGOOD: Sup people

VINCENTVG: Degas threatens to become a Graphic Artist. I spoke to him of the artist's responsibility. That which fills his head and heart must be expressed. He answers only with "A guy's gotta eat."

BUNNYHOP: How old are you HeavyMtl?

MAY 25

BUSINESS AND FINANCE CHAT ROOM, 10:12 A.M.

VINCENTVG: As you so warned, Gauguin is an intolerable presence as my roommate. Not only does he say my work is heavy and irrelevant, but he has taken to labeling all his provisions.

JDPOWER: Phizer Rizer!!!! Phizer Rizer!!!! Thanks for the new Porsche Viagra!!!!!!!!!!

GOLDMINE: Sally sells short by the seashore> Peter Picked a peck of Profit from the Pension Plan.

FANNIEMAE: You couldn't handle me tiger.

VINCENTVG: All is lost. Although I live lower than a beggar does, I am again without rations or funds. Instead of painting the sun as it radiated its brilliance on the field daisies, I spent the day deciding whether or not to eat my own foot. Whatever you can spare dear Theo...

GORDONG: The tumors are gone from the mice!! Ka-Ching!! Who's down with the pharmaceuticals!!

THEMAN: You need Viagra JD. All the limpdicks at Morgan need Viagra. Come to First Boston FannieMae. That's where the real men are!!

PHILJOHNSON: Does anyone know how I can cut my transaction fees? I'm paying up to 14 dollars per and I read somewhere that's high.

GOLDMINE: (To the tune of Stairway to Heaven) There's a lady I cold called, Who signed away all her life savings, and I'm Buuuyyyiiiinnng a condo in South Beeeaaaacchhhh!

VINCENTVG: Also, Theo, in response to your query last week, I made an effort to save on supplies by ordering over the Internet directly from the purveyor. The swines turned out to be simple pornographers and I was again pulled in by the ruse. I can assure you, dear Theo, the designation on your bill for "Hot Asian Backdoor Action" was not my intended transaction, although you were right to cancel my account.

JUNE 3

BEST LI'L CHATHOUSE, 3:44 P.M.

VINCENTVG: The sun Theo, the sun. Her name is FlyGrrrL69 and she's 26/f from Illinois. I know I once said that Love has the ebb and flood of the Sea, but at least the Sea won't sleep with your postman. Circumstances have changed. The cynicism of my depression has been replaced by a burgeoning twitch in my culottes.

TORINA56: any females out there want to talk

BABBY23: 16/m

SPINGLE2345: age 23/m

BADASS1212: HI room

TERMINATE2: Hey evryone

SCARYBAD: WHAT'S GOIN ON IN THIS ROOM

VINCENTVG: I was in a Nickelodeon chat room, making the argument that to mock the art of Thys Maris is to mock yourself. For Maris is the personification of all that is noble and others only regret that he hasn't been broken. While this fellow kept insisting that the first Darren on Bewitched was the finest Darren.

ANIMAL80: Sup.

Torina56: Nah much bro

JFL 44444: anybody out there

PPPPPUUU: DA DA DA

MMMan4U: Pics f?

SpinGle2345: Age/Sex?

VincentVG: Anyway, my angel chimed in "Vincent LOL." Do you know what that means Theo? LOL. Laugh out loud. You know yourself I've made no one laugh since my pants splitting incident at de Bock's opening exhibition at Rhine Station.

NEEDSEX: I jus got out a the pool

PPPPPUUU: 16/m

KruegerFred: 14/m

BIJohnson: 16/m

AnIMAL80: Any fine females want to chat 17/m

DaMASTER77: Hey people 43/m

SpinGle2345: *bad2bone*

VincentVG: Cursed finances. If you could see your way to passing on a couple of guilders it would be much anticipated. My newly beloved wants a pic and alas I have no scanner.

BUFF88dude: 15/m

JTHOMAS: 14/m michigan

XMAN2000: Sup people

JULY 12

MTV CHAT, 8:12 P.M.

RocKUWORL: Who hates Hanson press 11

AMBer22: WHOS COOL

RockSOLID: DOES ANYONE HAVE A MOLE IN A COOL PLACE

VincentVG: There comes a moment when all hope is lost, fatally and irrevocably, in the new foal that is budding romance. For me, it was finding out that my fair princess's AOL member profile turned out to be false.

KISSDAsky: 11

Tweddly44: 11

AssKIss33: i am

FERtillll: 11

ktttyyyy: me

Fkanchen: 11

VincentVG: My "26 year old, flaxen haired, full breasted, French schooled, bikini modeling, Ph.D. gymnast" turned out to be a lonely 57-year-old accountant named George, who is "into role playing." Alas I am crushed and humiliated.

DrTokeee: not u

FL67THat: IIIIIIIIIIIIIIIIIIIIIIIIIIIIIIIIIII

HAAAAAR22: HANSON IS A BUNCH OF HORNY BUT LOVING BROTHERS!!!!!!!!!!

AMBer22: How do u know

ALLGOOD55: I likey Metallica

FERtillll: alternatives

VincentVG: I poured my soul out to this fraudulent suitor. Not to mention that in my haste to impress my beloved with a poem, I accidentally cut off my ear and mailed it to her/him. I am the laughingstock of the entire electronic community, and rightfully so. My only Oasis is you dear brother . . . and the new modem you sent me.

JIFFpoppy: rap sux

Gra445Gri: I like them theyre sweet

TuTuTu33: anybody wanna chat?

Ton44Fgh: II dong diggity

Prapper: WUZ UP PEEPS

GREaaa69: II

VincentVG: I am through with painting. I will seek honest work. I am told of an Institute where a feeble failure such as myself can be redeemed to the world of the productive. It is called DeVry. If you could spare any morsel of currency it would be greatly appreciated. The courses do not come cheaply.

TOTalPack: Any hot grrrrls wanna cyber IM me

RuffRuff2: 11

VincentVG: Anyone here like Alanis Morrisette? press 22

Ton44Fgh: 22

Prapper: 22

JIFFpoppy: 22

REVENGE IS A DISH BEST
SERVED COLD

IT WOULDN'T BE long now.
Sheldon Stein sipped his Fresca. The bubbles tickled
his upper lip, as he had always dreamed they would. Sheldon wondered what his recently deceased mother would
think of this scene: Sheldon, feet up on his bastard of a
father's prized ottoman, swigging soda right from the can
while wearing a real turtleneck sweater. (Dickeys were for
suckers and Sheldon Stein had turned in his sucker cre-
dentials.) It would have killed her. If only the cursed natural
causes hadn't gotten her first. But Sheldon had waited thirty
years for this moment and was going to savor every delicious sensation. He took another decadent sip and giggled
with glee. The Hasbrook Heights Class of 1968 was gath-
ering tonight for its thirtieth high school reunion, unaware

of the hurricane poised to wreak havoc upon their tragically ordinary lives. A hurricane named Sheldon Francis Stein.

He smiled as he thumbed through a dog-eared copy of *Catcher in the Rye.* The Steins' paperboy, Sid, had let Sheldon borrow it some years ago, and in Sid's haste to go to college, become a doctor and have a family, he had foolishly forgotten to retrieve it. Sucker, Sheldon thought to himself. The book had provided a philosophical blueprint for this night's glorious triumph to be. Sheldon made a mental note to send word of his victory to the book's author, J. D. Salinger, just to let him know that at least one person "got it." Besides, he thought, this "Salinger" would probably be thrilled to hear from a fan. Sheldon made a quick list of excuses in case Salinger pursued a meeting upon getting his letter.

Sheldon's mood darkened, however, as he recalled the fateful move his parents made to this torturous community halfway through his senior year. He recalled his torment at the hands of his new classmates, their cruel taunts echoing in his mind.

"Excuse me, your name is Sheldon, right?" "Who do you have for biology, Sheldon?" "Hey, Sheldon, did you hear someone shot Bobby Kennedy?" Tears stung Sheldon's cheeks as he recalled the wretched echo of that name being hurled at him in the hallways of Hasbrook High. Hadn't he cried out for an end to their taunting? Hadn't he insisted on a nickname? Stinky had a nickname. Bubblebutt had a nickname. Whorey and Zitman too!! Even ol' Fuckface had a nickname. No, Sheldon was destined to spend his four months at Hasbrook without the renown and camaraderie only a nickname can bestow. But after tonight his chosen moniker would remain forever emblazoned in their minds. Sheldon glanced into his closet at the two T-shirts he had personalized for this glorious occasion. Would he go as the "Avenging Angel of Destruction"? Or would he go as "The Shellster"? Sheldon threw down the last of his Fresca and laughed the laugh of a man about to be born again. And then he coughed, as some of the delicious nectar went down the wrong pipe.

Sheldon's plan was a relatively simple one, as far as revenge schemes go. He ran through his final checklist. 1. Be rejected by the in crowd at your new high school. Check. 2. Wait thirty years to avenge anger, allowing for maximum surprise and preparation. Check. 3. Give yourself a nickname. Check. 4. Utilize science know-how to create a monster. Check. 5. Learn to drive. Check. 6. Drive monster to thirtieth reunion and unleash his horrible terror. All systems go, he thought, giddily borrowing terminology he recently had heard in an astronaut movie.

As Sheldon put the finishing touches on his potluck dish—all attendees of the reunion were required to bring one—he couldn't help but feel he was forgetting something. He filled the Tupperware container and reviewed the plan. Outcast, thirty years, monster . . . a cold chill came over him. Learn to drive!! In Sheldon's haste to create the monster he had completely overlooked step 5. He staggered to the bay window and stared longingly at the monolith that was Hasbrook High. Thirty years of planning and sacrifice lay in shambles on the shag carpet beneath his feet. Sheldon glanced at the clock. He had about twenty minutes to learn to drive or come up with an alternate plan. It briefly occurred to Sheldon that he might be able to lock all the exits to the reunion and create a firestorm inside, but that would require supernatural powers he didn't possess. He could egg their cars . . . but that seemed unworthy of a thirty-year plan. Perhaps if he had thought of it twenty-five years ago. NO. He had waited too long and worked too hard. He had to press on. If only Sheldon could convince the monster to walk the three blocks to the high school . . . and carry the drinks. Sheldon could bring the casserole and yearbook. They wouldn't need a car. It sounded crazy . . . but maybe crazy enough to work.

Sheldon stared at the padlocked door to his private basement laboratory. Beyond the door lay the fruit of his labor, the sleeping monster. He felt a curious mix of elation and trepidation, an emotional cocktail usually reserved for the nights he would steal a glimpse of *Baywatch* as his parents slept. But they were both gone now, and with them, the asthma attacks that had haunted his every waking moment. Sheldon hadn't hated his parents, but at times he'd resented their overprotective meddling. He recalled the years they had kept him in a plastic bubble after seeing a television movie about a boy with no immune system. They released him only after seeing the same boy starring in the movie *Grease.* His parents reasoned that if this boy Travolta was now healthy enough to sing and dance it might be safe to free Sheldon as well.

At least he had inherited some of the qualities he admired in his parents. From his father, a healthy curiosity about science and an obsessive need for revenge. And from his mother, the soft curves and pouty breasts that kept him from ever going swimming. He took a deep breath, unlocked the door and stepped down into the basement.

A single bulb backlit the frame of the monster, who seemed as peaceful in sleep as he was terrifying in his waking hours. Sheldon thought back to the day five years ago when he gave life to this powerful creature. The sacrifice, dedication and secrecy that had gone hand in hand with the project. His parents never knew. Sheldon had convinced them that his thousands of hours in the basement were spent masturbating. Botched experiments often made his lies more difficult, but his parents took to their graves the belief that sometimes when Sheldon ejaculated, there was an explosion and fire.

He remembered the setbacks and triumphs: The gene manipulation that created savage field mice—yet when applied to Rottweilers, made them go bald. The finger he had lost after giving life to a rabid slice of his mother's meat loaf. The broken nose he had suffered at the monster's bris. Sheldon regretted none of it. It had been a long hard road, but any worthy endeavor requires perseverance. Back when he was young, revenge required creativity and discipline, not like the kids today who have ready access to munitions and downloaded bomb recipes. Any twerp with a modem could do that. Sheldon swelled with pride as he reached out to his masterpiece.

Awakening the monster. This would be the most treacherous part. The monster wasn't what people would call "a morning person," and although it was nearly 8 P.M., Sheldon had to tread carefully. Act too abruptly, and the monster was liable to turn its venom upon its master. Too passive and it might never wake at all. Sheldon's hands trembled as he reached out toward the demon's lair. He shook the monster gently, taking care to whisper reassuringly, "Who wants ice cream?" Sheldon fell back as the monster's eyes shot open. Evil Incarnate blinked twice, looked over at Sheldon, yawned, and sat up.

They were out on the street. The late November air was cold and for a moment Sheldon thought maybe the personalized T-shirt wasn't such a good idea. He regretted not asking if he could get his nickname emblazoned on a sweatshirt instead. The man in the decal booth at the mall had been so abrupt. He glanced at the monster. He didn't look cold. Still, Sheldon swore revenge on the decal man. Sounds of the reunion floated down toward the pair. They were getting near their destination. Judgment Night was about to begin. It really was cold, though. Sheldon pressed on . . . and thought of soup.

Suddenly, through the darkness, a large man appeared in front of the duo, snapping Sheldon from his reverie. Sheldon realized they were still yards from their destination and moved to restrain the monster. The beast was too quick. In a flash it was on the man, moving with the destructive efficiency it was trained for. First one man, then another. Then what looked like a horse, and some very little men . . . and some sheep . . . and a baby. Sheldon had trouble keeping up as the bodies flew by. And then, as quickly as it had started, it was over. The monster stood alone in the killing fields, looking toward its master for approval. Sheldon smiled. "Excellent," he said, not wanting to hurt the monster's feelings. For he saw the man that had surprised them was a plastic Santa, and that the monster had destroyed the Wilkinsons' famous nativity and Christmas display. This, Sheldon knew, was bad. They hurried toward the reunion.

Soon they found themselves at the door to the gymnasium. In a moment Sheldon would harvest the fruit of all those years of torment. He turned to the behemoth. "It's time," he whispered, knowing that after their task was completed he would be saying goodbye to his only friend. The monster reached out his hand, the one Sheldon had made for him out of calciumized space-age polymers and leftover chicken, and wiped a tear from Sheldon's face. Sheldon turned away, not wanting the monster to see that because it lacked fine motor skills it had poked Sheldon in the eye. They walked in.

Sheldon was completely unprepared for the scene that greeted his triumphant arrival. The reunion he had waited thirty years to destroy had already fallen victim to chaos and mayhem. As the stereo played "The End," the class of '68's prom theme, Sheldon stood dumbfounded. Up on the podium Little James McKlelland, Sheldon's only classmate with one leg shorter than the other, stood glassy-eyed, six sticks of dynamite taped to his chest. "Goiter Gail" Johnson, the girl Sheldon sat next to in geometry, was perched on the lighting grid, firing what appeared to be a homemade laser gun. A man Sheldon couldn't quite place was flying around the room in a jet pack, throwing Chinese death

stars at the petrified revelers. Sheldon quickly discovered
the would-be celebrants were far outnumbered by those
seeking vindication. He counted only eleven or twelve people in formalwear, while the other hundred or so sported
hats and T-shirts ranging in declarations from I WILL NOT
BE IGNORED to THE GLEE CLUB CAN GO FUCK THEMSELVES. A
man wearing a NIGHT OF RECKONING T-shirt stomped past
Sheldon and angrily threw a carton of eggs in the trash.
The monster seemed disappointed as well, like a child who
was told he was going to Willie Wonka's only to end up
in church. It tugged on Sheldon's shirt and tried to mouth
"Home now" through the opening in its face that Sheldon
had carved with a melon baller.

"Hello, Sheldon." Sheldon spun in the direction of the
voice. It was Beth Ann Dunwoody, the prom queen. "How
are you?" she purred. Something was very wrong here. Sheldon was sure Beth Ann hadn't even known he was alive in
high school. Why was she talking to him? Why was seaweed draped over her naked, wet body? Why did her face
look melted? He remembered she had mysteriously disap-
peared down by the lake during the summer of '68. "You
haven't seen J. T. or Tommy Mullens here, have you? I
want to talk to them about our little skinny-dipping date,"
she said, brandishing a large, rusted ice hook. "Uh . . .
well . . ." Sheldon glanced uncomfortably around the room.
"I think they're hiding under table six," he said, hating the
way he stammered around pretty girls. "Thanks. You're a
doll," she said as she sloshed off toward her target. The
monster giggled. "What are you laughing at?" Sheldon
asked. The monster shrugged. Sheldon grabbed the beast

and turned back toward the exit as a canister of anthrax exploded by the chin-up bars to their left. "Let's get out of here," he said, checking his watch. "*Baywatch* is on in half an hour." The monster clapped happily as they walked out into the night.

ADOLF HITLER:
THE LARRY KING INTERVIEW

ONE OF THE beautiful aspects of our culture is the capacity we have to forgive, especially those in the public eye. There is little a tearful mea culpa on *60 Minutes* or a tell-all confession in the pages of *People* magazine won't rectify. This grand compassion was put to the ultimate challenge when in the fall of 1999 an astonished world watched as a historical figure long thought to have died in World War II resurfaced. This disgraced dictator, swayed by a beautifully arranged fruit basket and handwritten note, went on CNN's *Larry King Live*. The Hitler interview, as it became known, aired on October 23, 1999, at 10:00 P.M. Eastern Standard Time. That night King's ratings tripled, allowing his show to narrowly defeat all other cable entries airing in that time slot, as well as the WB sitcom *Whassup Skinnybones Jones*, the story of a skinny black man living among fatter, funnier black men. The following is an uncensored transcript of that historic interview.

KING: Good evening, ladies and gentlemen. Tonight we bring you perhaps the most controversial show in the history of *Larry King Live*. He began his career as president of the fledgling National Socialist party, the Nazi party, in Germany. After a failed coup, some prison time and a bestselling book, he reestablished himself in the German hierarchy, first as chancellor ... then as Führer. The next ten years under his watch saw Germany's return to power, shame at the Munich Olympics, a failed marriage and finally, one helluva World War complete with what was thought to be a cowardly demise by his own hand. Tonight, risen from the proverbial dead, we welcome Adolf Hitler.

HITLER: (*biting into a bagel*) First of all, Larry, I don't know what I was so afraid of. These are delicious!!!

KING: Well, Chancellor Hitler, I have—

HITLER: Please call me Adolf.

KING: Adolf. First of all, I have to say ... quite frankly, we were very reluctant to have you on.

HITLER: I can't say I blame you for that. I mean, you hear the name Hitler ...

KING: Well, in the end we decided this show is about newsmakers. That's been my motto through forty years of broadcasting and critics be damned, I'm not about to stop now.

HITLER: I don't know what you're talking about.

KING: What do you say to all the people out there, the people who view you as a demon, the perpetrator of the most vicious—

HITLER: Guilty as charged, Larry. Look, I was a bad guy. No question. *I* hate that Hitler. The yelling, the finger pointing, I don't know... I was a very angry guy.

KING: And this... new Hitler?

HITLER: I get up at seven, have half a melon, do the Jumble in the morning paper and then let the day take me where it will. Some days I'll fish, maybe hit the mall for an Orange Julius. The other day I spent seven hours in the park watching ants cart off part of a sandwich. Me!! The inventor of the Blitzkrieg... When you stop having to control everything, it's very freeing.

KING: Why did you do it?

HITLER: Whooo boy. The $64,000 question. I don't know... I wasn't a happy kid. I mean, I'm not trying to make excuses, but you go through high school with one testicle and the nickname Shitler... I'm sorry, they can bleep that, right?

KING: It's fine.

HITLER: After a while you get sick of it. One day you just snap. It started out as the typical "Someday you guys will be sorry," and then...I don't know. It just got away from me.

KING: Did you ever see the despicable nature of your actions? Was there any remorse?

HITLER: Oh sure, but denial is a powerful thing...I always thought I could stop any time I wanted. "If I could just get Czechoslovakia, that'll be the end of it. I'll be happy then." And I'd get it and think, well geez, Poland's just up the road a piece and...you know the rest. I think admitting to myself that there was a problem was the toughest part.

KING: And when was that?

HITLER: Well...I'm not going to lie to you, it took a while. There were moments all along where I knew something was wrong. I remember one time...I think it was in Munich. We were having a rally. 100,000 people all chanting my name. The bonfires were going. The whole shebang. It should've been a crowning moment but I clearly remember thinking, What am I doing here? I hate crowds.

KING: And when was that?

HITLER: I believe that was in 1942. But I didn't hit rock bottom until, as you know, 1945.

KING: Yes, tell us about those final days in the Berlin bunker, where, until now, we had assumed you had killed yourself.

HITLER: (*takes a sip of water*) Right, well. Funny story. Everyone thought I went into the bunker to escape...

KING: Not the case?

HITLER: No. Actually, as the Allied Forces were closing in I was still in denial. I really thought we were gonna rally, you know, make an end run around Switzerland and flank 'em. So I'm planning furiously and snapping at people—as my therapist says, "playing the dictator." So Eva calls me down to the bunker for some "emergency" with the generators. Anyway, I go down and there's Eva and Himmler and two of my other closest friends. I'll never forget. I walk in and say *"Was ist los?"* And Eva takes my face in her hands, looks me in the eyes and says "Adolf, we all love you very much, but if you don't stop with this conquer and purify thing, no one in this room will ever talk to you again."

KING: And that snapped you out of it?

HITLER: Not quite. You have to understand I'd been running with this thing for about fifteen years at that point.

KING: What happened?

HITLER: I shot them. Back then we didn't know from interventions. I just figured they were betraying me.

Anyway, I threw on Eva's clothes and snuck out into the night. I lived like an animal for weeks, doing what I had to do to get by. One day a group of boys were making fun of the lady with the mustache, and I got a look at myself in the reflection of a window and realized they were talking about me. It was then I knew I had to get my life together.

KING: Interesting. Now tell me about your relationship with Eva. She was a beautiful woman. Do you think she was mesmerized by your power?

HITLER: What are you insinuating?

KING: I'm just saying she seemed like a lovely gal and—

HITLER: You think she was only into me because I was the Führer? You think I conquered half of Europe and killed untold millions just to get laid?

KING: No, I was merely—

HITLER: Well, all I can say is (*breaks into a broad smile*) yes to the first part and amen brother to the second. (*King looks confused.*) Look, Larry. I learned long ago that Bavarian art majors with oily hair and weasely mustaches weren't getting the ladies. Of course that was the only reason Eva went out with me. Women love power and fame. How many times have you been married, Larry?

KING: Ummm. Seven, maybe eight. But this last one is for life. I love my Shawnie . . .

HITLER: Right. Anyway, my point is you've married a lot of very beautiful women. And quite frankly, your own physical presence is ... how do I put this ... mildly disturbing. I mean, if you were Larry King the nice guy who ran a dry cleaner's, you and the former Ida Klinghoff of Canarsie would be heading toward your fiftieth wedding anniversary right about now. Right or wrong? (*King is dumbfounded.*) No offense, mind you.

KING: Let's go to the phones.... Annie from Grand Rapids, Michigan, what's your question for Adolf Hitler?

ANNIE: First of all, Larry, I love your show.

KING: Thank you.

ANNIE: My husband was recently diagnosed with shingles and your show is the only thing that takes away the itching.

KING: Wonderful, Annie, thank you. What's your question for Hitler?

ANNIE: Yes, I want to know what Mr. Hitler thinks of cloning?

(*Hitler smiles.*)

KING: Terrific question. Scientists recently cloned a sheep ... Dolly I believe was her name. You've always had an interest in things genetic. Your take on this scientific breakthrough.

HITLER: Well, Larry, "transgenics," as that branch of genetic research is known, is an exciting specialty, and the Roslin project, the sheep cloning, is an exciting advance. But I certainly wouldn't qualify it as a breakthrough.

KING: So your passion for science is undimmed.

HITLER: (*a little defensive*) Well, passion, yes, but not obsession. Part of my growth has come in recognizing compulsive tendencies and dealing with them in a proactive manner. For instance, yes, I spend a bit of time immersed in genetic research, but I've also invaded the world of ballroom dancing. And this fall I'll begin mastering the musical frailties of the French horn.

KING: You must admit there are real ethical questions that go along with the cloning of humans?

HITLER: Well, Larry, let's call a spade a spade. The big fear here is that some evil guy gets a hold of this stuff and makes another me. I mean, as early as the seventies they were making horror movies about it.

KING: *The Boys from Brazil.* For my money Sir Larry Olivier never shined brighter. We had him on and—

HITLER: (*pointedly*) Well, I never saw the movie, I'm happy to say. Although friends told me not only were the performances thin, it was too long! But, Larry, getting back on point, people will never be cloned. Superficially perhaps, but personality, character, even intelligence cannot be genetically duplicated. Only tendencies. I'm a big environment convert. Nurture over nature. You could duplicate my genes, but you wouldn't get *me* unless you duplicate *my* upbringing. You'd have to get some older children to tease this new Hitler mercilessly, giving him constant wedgies . . . ripping the only pair of . . . lederhosen . . . I loved those . . . (*Hitler begins to cry.*) Excuse me, I believe some dust is in my contacts. (*Hitler wipes his eyes.*)

KING: Was the Third Reich working on cloning?

HITLER: (*sips some water*) Oh, sure, we gave it a shot. We had created some chickens that vaguely resembled each other. And one of our top guys had cloned a replica of your heroic dog Lassie—but after some checking we found out it was just a reassembled corgi. All involved were put to sleep. Our guys just weren't up to the task.

KING: You had certainly made science a priority . . .

HITLER: Which brings up an interesting irony, Larry. Here I was, a guy with a plan to create a master race, dominate the world by blending brute force with cutting-edge technology. So what do I do? I *deport* or *kill* all my best scientists. Huh? Do you see? The Jews were some of my best technical people. (*Larry looks puzzled.*) It's classic fear of success. I create something, then sabotage its chances of ever actually working. It's a pattern I've repeated over and over again. I'm defeating all challengers on the Western front, couple more weeks, I got the whole thing sewn up. So what do *I* do? Attack Russia?!! (*Hitler taps his finger on his temple.*) Way to go, genius!! Seems obvious, but these insights came very slowly to me.

KING: But you got away with it. After all these years, why resurface and open yourself up to the incredible tumult your return has created?

HITLER: Stay off the radar? No, that's a good question. See, I had been talking a good game for many years now. What a changed man I was, how I'd found real peace, but I was still playing the blame game. My therapist challenged me to put up or shut up. To prove to myself that I could take responsibility for my life. So here I am.

KING: (*holding up a book*) We've been talking with Adolf Hitler, the book is—

HITLER: Is it over already?

KING: I'm afraid so.

HITLER: Wow, that was fast. I thought I was the one who had ways of making *you* talk. (*Both laugh.*) But seriously, the book is called *Mein Comfortable Shoes*—get it?

KING: I do.

HITLER: It's about an angry man who learns to appreciate the little things in life. It's about acceptance.

KING: And it's a terrific read. Folks, if you read no other book this summer, make it *Mein Comfortable Shoes.*

HITLER: Thank you, Larry.

KING: And what's next for Adolf Hitler?

HITLER: I'll be doing *Politically Incorrect* next Thursday, and as always you can see my old work on the A&E network, every night following Bud Friedman's *An Evening at the Improv.*

KING: Lovely man, Bud Friedman, very funny.

HITLER: Yes indeed. And as you know, in two weeks, I'll be appearing on Court TV as I stand trial for crimes against humanity.

KING: Right, that is coming up. What kind of defense will you be offering?

HITLER: Not much. I fully expect that by this time next year, I'll have been convicted and possibly put to death. I'm going to represent myself, though. From now on the blame goes here (*pointing to chest*). The only one to blame for Hitler . . . is Hitler. Besides, who wants to get involved with a bunch of phony baloney defense lawyers . . . I mean, talk about evil. (*Both laugh.*)

KING: Well, Adolf, thanks for coming by.

HITLER: Thank you.

KING: (*to camera*) Coming up after the break, Loni Anderson: She's fifty, she's in a new relationship with a younger man and she's not apologizing. Loni Anderson with her new book, *Fifty, a Younger Man and Not Apologizing,* after the break.

LENNY BRUCE:
THE MAKING OF A SITCOM

DATE: Dec. 3, 1960
FROM: F. Silverman Prod. Asst.
TO: J. Aubrey VP Programming, ABC
RE: Talent Search—The Crescendo in Hollywood

Saw the Four Freshmen at the Crescendo. Thought they
might make for a funny high school sitcom, but found out
they weren't actually freshmen. Opening act was interesting.
Lenny Bruce. Hilarious. Didn't see him perform but word
at the club is he won't be there long. And this was only
his first night! I guess he's a comer. Better jump before
NBC or CBS gets him. Could be our answer for Danny
Thomas or Benny.

DATE: Jan. 23, 1961
FROM: F. Silverman Prod. Coordinator
TO: L. Goldenson, President ABC, J. Warner, President
   Warner Bros., J. Aubrey VP Programming ABC, D. Lewine
   VP Programming ABC.
RE: Minutes of the Jan. Meeting on the Lenny Bruce Sitcom
   development project

Bruce meeting went very well. I do believe this is our guy.
Not crazy about Lenny's original suggestion of a show
about a Jewish Davy Crockett with a coonskin yarmulke,
although we could give further consideration to the mar-
keting aspects. My opinion is that kids won't buy coonskin
yarmulkes, even if we call them beanies, as Mr. Bruce sug-
gested.

   Jack Warner's suggestion of a sitcom to reflect Lenny's
reality is a winner. Audiences buy it because it's real. Aubrey's idea of playing up the war veteran angle of Bruce's
life is also a winner. We haven't seen a funny Audie Murphy yet so the timing could be perfect. Especially if we set
the show in Nebraska and add three-year-old twins as Mr.
Goldenson said.

   I think Lenny was won over. Especially when he found
out the kind of talent we can surround him with here at
ABC. I told him in the hallway that we've got producer
Hal Roach Jr. and designer Edith Head under contract. He
said if we could get him a Roach and Head, or even just
Head, he'd be a happy camper.

   I also checked into Mr. Warner's concern about

Lenny's itching and nodding off during the meeting. Mr. Bruce's personal physician, a Dr. Slats Finnegan of Miami, assured me the symptoms would disappear after adjusting Mr. Bruce's allergy medicine. Still looking for that tape of Mr. Bruce's act. His agent, Jack Sobel, said he sent it over but I have yet to track it down.

DATE: April 11, 1961
TO: L. Bruce
FROM: F. Silverman VP Programming
    Development ABC
RE: Lenny Bruce project pilot script

First off, Mr. Bruce, let me congratulate you on the punctual delivery of your pilot script. Some of the cocktail napkins weren't entirely legible, but we were able to get the general idea. It's very funny, although the *Make Room for Daddy* writers we assigned to the project said it was not exactly the same script as the one they thought was being turned in. Irregardless of the high quality of your work, the "suits" as always, have a couple of nitpicks we should go over.

THE TITLE: Because the show is to take place in Nebraska we feel it's best to go back to Jack Warner's original idea for a title, *Have a Heartland.* We felt the title *Schmucks* doesn't brand a clear enough image of the warmth and humor we all know this show will possess. Besides, a quickie poll of the gals in the secretarial pool showed a good 85% thought schmucks was a breakfast food.

YOUR CHARACTER: We applaud the "up-and-coming comedian" aspect to your character. It's real and gives the audience a chance to identify with and root for the underdog in all of us. In the pilot, however, your character never deals with this very fertile area. We never see him at work or even talking about work.

Also, your character has no visible or legal means of supporting the family while pursuing this worthwhile dream. Your character's dialogue (on the second "Hungry I" napkin), "Here I am digging the priest scam. A Jew boy from Brooklyn conning old Catholic gals out of their pensions on the promise of an eternal bliss without liver spots. But it's only enough scratch for a taste" is a start. Rather than a con artist, however, we thought your character could be an elementary school teacher. Remember, these suggestions are just food for your brain.

YOUR BEST FRIEND: This idea leads into the next character, your best friend, "Flat Foot Jackson—an uptown sax hipster who could blow cheese that made the Virgin Mary cum in her golden panties." Although jazz is certainly gaining in popularity, we thought perhaps this character might work better at the elementary school, as its wise yet sometimes overlooked custodian. And while we appreciate that Flat Foot's character is the best cook in Harlem, we'd prefer if there is to be cooking on the show, that your wife do it. And what exactly is a Dilaudid casserole with Methedrine sprinkles?

YOUR WIFE: Given only your character description of "a sweet-faced shiksa dancer, with big tits and magnificent pink nipples," we agree that Angie Dickinson could work. We need, however, more description. Two other things. What kind of dancer is she? And although we love the endearing quality of you referring to her as "Honey," at some point in the process, we'll need to know her actual name.

YOUR DAUGHTER: We love the idea of the daughter character. We want to see more of her. Actually, we would like to see any of her. Why, if she is your daughter, does she live with your mother? We can all appreciate that "pimps and whores do not playmates make," but perhaps our school idea will solve that riddle, and the daughter can come home. Also, why do you and your wife live in a flophouse?

THE PLOT: We don't, under any circumstances, think you should cheat on your wife in the pilot episode, especially when she's just been arrested. We agree that her character is certainly in the wrong after "copping my ten grand and turning on every freak in Hollywood" and agree that she seems to treat you "like shit." This still doesn't justify your character's indifference to her arrest as stated on the third "Playboy Club" napkin, "That fucking hillbilly whorehouse junkie bitch can feast on prison cuisine. Dyke sandwiches for everyone!"

We were thinking that instead of the episode centering around Honey's betraying you and her second-act arrest on prostitution and drug charges, perhaps she could be nagging you for a new car. But you've got your eyes on a state-of-the-art television set.

Also, the B story involving the character of "White Man" could be tweaked. It's an amusing runner to have him constantly making sure that the "sheeny and negro promise not to put it to my sister" but we thought maybe he just wants to borrow your lawnmower. Also we thought it would be nice to give him a name other than "White Man." Ned, perhaps. And he shouldn't be drinking.

Overall I think we're off to a great start. We're all really excited about this project and believe with some integration of a few of the abovementioned notes, we have a real winner here. Look forward to your thoughts.

DATE: April 14, 1961
FROM: F. Silverman Vice President ABC
TO: L. Bruce
RE: Script notes and rewrite

Let me begin, Mr. Bruce, by saying how surprised and pleased we all were here at the American Broadcasting Company by the alacrity of your response to our script notes. Contractually you were not required to tender a second draft of your pilot script until June I, yet you seem to have turned one around in less than twenty-four hours. So . . . Bravo!

On the other hand, your redraft seems not to address

a few of our concerns. While we may have appeared overly critical in our notes concerning your first draft, our intent was to help you continue polishing that effort. The emerging view of your current work is that you are now working on a completely different project. And while we can agree this new project is quite entertaining, we were wondering what happened to all the other characters and plot points we had originally discussed.

If we are correct in piecing together the balled-up cigarette papers this draft was submitted on, it seems you are now working on a pilot script entitled *The Lone Ranger Is a Fag*. If that is correct, Mr. Bruce, I must make you aware of ABC's strenuous objection. A masked man fighting crime as the Lone Ranger is a wonderful idea, but unfortunately one that already exists—first on radio and then as a very successful television program. The legal eagles here at ABC have asked me to make it clear that we do not condone plagiarism in any form. We must officially state that if you are committed to this *Lone Ranger Is a Fag* script we will no longer be able to continue our involvement in the project.

If you would, however, permit us to change the name of the lead character from the Lone Ranger to the "Single Horseman," we might have interest in pursuing this new script. We all very much liked the crime-fighting angle. Also we would prefer if you would change this Single Horseman character into a heterosexual. This small change would fix the Single Horseman's currently problematic relationship with his partner in crime fighting, the Indian Tonto. Whom we would now like you to call Ronto.

Again, Mr. Bruce, please just take these suggestions as bricks to help you build . . . buildings.

Oh, and before I forget: You mistakenly enclosed a grainy black-and-white photograph in the envelope with your script. It is, I believe, a picture of a woman checking her dog's genitals for ticks, using what appears to be her mouth. The scribbled inscription says, "Greetings from Miss America" and also that the dog's name is Fred. I am sending it back to you with the hope that its disappearance caused you no worry, as I imagine it may have sentimental value.

DATE: May 11, 1961
FROM: F. Silverman, President, ABC
TO: Jack Sobel, agent and attorney for L. Bruce
RE: The incident

It is with great regret we must inform you of the termination of Mr. Bruce's contract with the American Broadcasting Company. We understand he had some issues with the creative process, but we don't feel it was handled appropriately. The circus atmosphere he created by showing up at our offices naked made it nearly impossible to focus on his grievances. We do apologize for his untimely fall from our third-floor window. Our security can be overly zealous.

I can also assure Mr. Bruce that I was not spawned from an unholy tryst involving Senator McCarthy and Mother Cabrini. My people are actually from Massapequa. Good luck in your future endeavors.

•   •   •

The untitled Lenny Bruce project was subsequently sold to CBS. It was assigned to Sheldon Leonard and on October 3, 1961, it debuted as The Dick Van Dyke Show. *Lenny Bruce died on August 3, 1966. At the time of his death he was working on a pilot for a children's show about the perils of our legal system called* Uncle Lenny's Guide to All Things Penal. *The show was set for a fall slot on ABC.*

MICROSOFT WORD '98 SUGGESTED SPELLING AND USAGE

IF, DURING THE reading of this book, you found yourself confused by certain language and usage, you are not alone. In fact the computer program I used to write the book often argued vehemently with me over some of my choices. Here is a list of the words that were problematic as well as the computer's suggestions. Feel free to go back and replace the words I used with the computer's corrections.

ME, WRONG	MICROSOFT SUGGESTION
Kaftan-	CAFTAN
Caftan-	KAFTAN
Wilford Brimley-	WILLARD BRAMBLY

Moishe the Barback-	MOIST THE BAREBACK, MOOCH THE BARRACK
Portnoy's Complaint-	PORTION'S COMPLAINT, PROTON'S COMPLAINT
J. D. Salinger-	J. D. SLANDER
Web site-	WEBSTER
Fellating-	FELTING
Whupped-	WHAPPED, WHIPPED, WHOOPED
Jewey-	DEWEY
Geraldo-	GERALD
Kathie Lee Gifford-	KATHY LEE GIFFORD
Barbra Streisand-	BARBARA STREISAND
Ozzy Ozborne-	OOZY OZBORNE
Jerry Seinfeld-	JERRY SNIFFLED, JERRY SNIVELED
Carrot Top-	CARTOON
Davy Crockett-	DAVY CROCKER
Lenny Bruce-	LEANNE BRUCE, LEONINE BRUCE
Schmuck-	SCHICK, SCHLOCK, SCHECK
Yid-	ID, YIN, YIP
Shiksa-	SHEIKS, SHAKES
Oy Vey-	OYO VERY, OXY VEX
Tu padre tiene mucho pelo en su pinga-	TU PADRE TINE MUCH PAELLA SUE PINGS

Ay Caramba-	ET CARMAKER, AYE CRUMB
Shitler-	TILTER, HITLER, WHITTLER
Loni Anderson-	LOIN ANDERSON, LOON ANDERSON
Caligula-	COLLEGIAL
Hyannis Port-	HYENAS PORT
Mr. Feelyhands-	NO SUGGESTIONS
Fuckface-	NO SUGGESTIONS
Cocksucker-	NO SUGGESTIONS
Chickenshit-	NO SUGGESTIONS
Alan Dershowitz-	NO SUGGESTIONS
Der Führer-	DOUR FURRIER
Cockblock-	CHOCKABLOCK
John Tesh-	JOHN TECH, JOHN TEST
Bennigans-	BENIGN
Dachau-	DASH, DASHER
Harpo Marx-	HARPOON MARX
Fuckee Suckee-	FUQUA SUCKLE
Leonid Brezhnev-	LEANED BERGEN
Al Haig-	AL HAG, AL HAIR
Henry Kissinger-	HENRY KISSING, HENRY COSIGNER